A GUIDE T
MUSIC EDU

Editor-in-chief **Graeme Kay**

Editor **Helen Wallace**

Sub-editor **Anna Tims**

Designer **Sue Holmes**

Illustrations **Adrian Nicholls**

Advertising **David Etherington, Natalie Ringe**

Production Controller **Mark Reeves**

Acknowledgements

With grateful thanks to those who gave their invaluable
time and expertise in the making of this book: John Stephens,
Gill Graham, Julia Freeman, David and Gillian Victor-Smith,
David Murphy, Hugh Benham, Steve Lewis, David Kettle

Published by BBC Books,
an imprint of BBC Worldwide Publishing,
BBC Worldwide Limited, Woodlands,
80 Wood Lane, London W12 0TT
Enquiries 0181 576 3283/3693, fax 0181 576 3292

First published 1998

© BBC Music Magazine

ISBN 0563 384 387

Colour reproduction by Pace Colour, Unit 6, Chevron Business Park,
Holbury, Southampton SO45 2QL
Printed and bound in Great Britain by Clays Ltd, St Ives plc

Cover pictures: Charles Thatcher–Tony Stone, Pictor International, Dan Burn Forti
Back cover: Johanna Mungo

Handbook of

usic awards &

Scholarships

1998/1999

This publication gives
details of nearly 200 music awards
and scholarships and is available now.
To order your copy please write, with
a cheque for £5.50,
made payable to
Music Education Fund,
to Awards & Trusts Administrator
16 Ogle Street, London W1P 8JB

MUSICIANS
BENEVOLENT FUND

CONTENTS

Contributors

ANDREW GREEN
is a former teacher and
concert agent, a father
of two and presents
music programmes for
BBC Radio 3 & 4

AMANDA HOLLOWAY
is former chief
sub-editor of *BBC Music
Magazine*. She has two
sons at St George's
Windsor choir school

KATE JONES is a
flautist, singer and music
publicist. She is training
as a music counsellor

ELESTR LEE
is a violinist, teacher
and writer

ROBERT MAYCOCK
is a music writer for the
Independent, *BBC Music
Magazine* and many
other publications, and
is a member of South
East Arts Board

KATE SHERRIFF is a
music writer and
sub-editor on *BBC
Music Magazine*

GAVIN THOMAS
is a composer

ANNA TIMS is the
former arts editor of
the *European*

HELEN WALLACE is
deputy editor of *BBC
Music Magazine* and a
Times critic. She is also
a qualified cello teacher

Introduction

Why sparing the bow might spoil the child

THE MOTHER of a talented musical friend of mine used to relate how she first asked her ten-year-old offspring if he'd like to learn the piano. 'Will it take more than 15 minutes?' was the response.

That was the late Fifties. You hardly need me to remind you that kids of today are likely to be considerably more impatient ('Will it take more than five minutes?') given that the range of distractions has increased dramatically. Against all the competition from videos and computer games, mountain bikes, discos and designer clothes – oh, and ever-earlier girl- and boyfriends – music lessons and the dreaded 'P' word, Practice, can seem the tamest options for those apparently (so the younger generation argues) fleeting moments of free time. So fleeting that (am I alone in observing this?) even flushing the loo can barely be fitted into the schedule.

This short book is not designed just for parents fighting against such odds, let me hasten to add. I hope it will prove just as useful to those with musically motivated children. Whatever the gloom merchants may say, every week tens of thousands of eager youngsters continue to put in willing effort in order to reap the pleasure of making music in all sorts of contexts. There is much imaginative, exciting and ground-breaking work being put in by gifted and dedicated teachers and musicians across the country. This is something to be celebrated and cherished. But at the same time these are, in many ways, particularly difficult times in which to help a child develop a continuing interest in making music, not least – as you will regularly read in what follows – because of significant threats to the provision of music tuition in schools in many parts of the country and the government's decision that music should no longer be compulsory in primary schools.

If music has often been the loser when challenged by the myriad distractions that children face these days, changing relationships within the family have also, perhaps, had a part to play. Many parents today feel uncomfortable about the idea of imposing themselves on their children in ways that would have been regarded as normal and proper 40 years ago. Children are more willing to express forthright opinions in front of their parents. No bad thing, we might argue, but when it comes to music you get the sneaking impression that there are many mothers and fathers for whom the memory of being dragooned into playing an instrument is the very symbol of what the anti-authority rebellion of the Sixties and Seventies was all about – never mind Vietnam and apartheid.

Parents I speak to often make it clear that they wish their children to have complete freedom of choice over whether or not to start – and pursue – a musical instrument. Often the result seems to be that the child in question dabbles in the clarinet or violin for a month or two, gets bored and then is allowed to give it up, maybe or maybe not moving on to another passing enthusiasm. With more parents in paid employment away from the home than ever before, the effort to keep a child involved with the regular round of music practice can seem positively purgatorial – and no competition for a stiff gin and *Brookside* after you've come through the front door. Is there a better way?

I count myself in the ranks of those who regret the decision made (at the age of eight) to give up the piano almost as soon as I had begun. By the age of 15, when the enthusiasm resurfaced, it was a touch late to make the most of whatever it was I had, as my long-suffering friends will confirm. Just as in so many fields, sporting and academic, early groundwork is highly desirable (if not essential – late starters take note) if latent talent is really to flourish. And that is going to make demands on parents in some way or other. Not least in the area of making choices for our children (there, I've said it!). Following those choices through means being engaged in sensitive and practical measures that help the child to understand that enjoyment and a sense of achievement outweigh the hard work involved. If a child has demonstrable musical talent, then going along with his or her freedom of choice unquestioningly may actually deny them freedom of choice in adulthood – the freedom to choose all the added pleasure that actually participating in music to a good standard can bring.

Which is, we hope, where this book comes in. Maybe you have an interest in music yourself, maybe you don't; in either case, if you want to learn more about your child's musical potential and help him or her to realise it, then we have tried to isolate the key choices that need to be made right from the start and the strategies for making the business of mastering an instrument seem a little more like fun. What instrument will best suit his or her particular talent and personality? What are the different methods for teaching that instrument? What qualities should I be looking for in a teacher? How can I help with practice – even when I don't play an instrument myself? What are the options if my child turns out to have an above average talent that needs special nurturing? How can I keep him or her musically occupied during the school holidays? Are exams necessary? What careers lie at the end of the process?

What is increasingly clear is that music-making is not an activity set apart from the mainstream of life. A growing body of research suggests that an engagement with music benefits the general process of learning in childhood. However, as I write these words the *Times Educational Supplement* has just published the results of a major survey showing, among other things, that the provision of instrumental tuition in our schools is under serious threat, especially as far as children from less well-off families are concerned. The days when there was a piano in every home and a sing-song or recital after supper every night are long since gone. But the world needs the music – and the next generation of musicians – as much as ever.

Andrew Green, May 1998

1. Is your child musical?

Motivation over musical genius

GUSTAV HOLST may have composed *The Planets*, but his feet were planted squarely on *terra firma* as far as music education was concerned. For years he carried out the day-to-day work of a schoolteacher at St Paul's School for Girls in Hammersmith. His practical experience, it's said, was that any child could be cured of so-called 'tone-deafness' given a course of daily five-minute lessons. Somewhere in the BBC's sound archive is the legendary, glowing testimonial to the work of another inner city music teacher who worked miracles on her so-called 'hopeless' pupils. Recorded before she set to work, their singing voices wouldn't have passed muster on any football terrace in England. After her training they sang as sweetly as cathedral choirboys.

The lesson is not simply that there's a cure for singing out of tune, but that children shouldn't be written off musically on the basis of rough, rule-of-thumb judgements. Sure, noticing that Julie or James sing along to the building society adverts on television in tune and in rhythm is a perfectly valid starting point for deciding that they have a talent worth exploring. But educationalists these days are increasingly reluctant to place children in 'musical' and 'non-musical' categories, not least on the evidence of their singing voices. 'In the past there were quite a few tests which set out to measure musical ability,' says Sue Hallam of the Institute of Education in London. 'They're still occasionally used, but in general terms there's now far less confidence that we can define what being "musical" actually is. You can test a child's ear for sound, but in fact you need a range of different skills to tackle an instrument.'

Research carried out at Keele University has suggested that more caution should even be exercised in using such loaded terms as 'genius' or 'natural talent'. Motivation and practice are, it's said, the key elements that lie behind musical success. 'Music pervades our world and we all react to it,' says David Vinden, a lecturer at London's Trinity College of Music. 'Most people can and do appreciate music in some way or other. The question to me is not "Is my child musical?", but "Do I appreciate the part music can play in my child's development?".'

According to Mike Weipert, general manager of the North East Music Co-operative in Newcastle, which provides musical tuition and activities in the Tyneside region: 'Parents often think that if their child can't sing in tune then they're not musical. Well, Evelyn Glennie can't hear pitch at all, but you'd hardly say she isn't musical. It's perfectly normal for a child to work gradually towards a precise sense of pitch.'

Character building

Acquiring even basic musical skills helps children in a range of ways, says Mike Weipert. Good training in singing or playing an instrument brings self-confidence and self-respect. 'Any skill in which you invest time and effort becomes important to you. Conversely, being written off when young can have a devastating effect.'

The spin-offs from developing musical ability extend into other areas – enhancing physical co-ordination, for example, and improving academic skills such as numeracy and literacy simply by virtue of learning how to read music. 'Sadly,' says Weipert, 'many schools fail to see this. In the inner city areas of my region 95 per cent of children don't turn up for the audition that we offer to show them what musical activity they could become involved in. Yet these are kids who aren't musically illiterate at all. They know plenty of pop music from the radio and discos. My view is that if we don't develop a child's appreciation of the arts then we can't say we're developing the whole person.'

Researchers are increasingly taking seriously the idea that music can enhance learning at the subconscious level, apparently stimulating the brain in ways that, as yet, cannot be fully understood. Work carried out

ACTION POINTS

● Motivation and practice rather than genius are key factors of musical success

● Even basic music skills can help build self-confidence and self-respect and improve numeracy and literacy

● If your school can't help, find out the provision in your area through the Federation of Music Services

● Specialist music schools and junior departments at conservatoires will assess gifted children and offer advice

● Research suggests music can help those with special needs and several organisations advise on this

recently at Oxford University, for example, found that eight- and nine-year-old pupils showed improved results in a series of spelling, arithmetic and spatial reasoning tests after listening to Mozart's piano music for ten minutes before each. The findings, presented at the British Psychological Society's 1998 conference, were built on existing research at the University of California and elsewhere. The signs are intriguing – not least in the work of science teacher Anne Savan at Aberdare Boys' Comprehensive School in South Wales. Playing Mozart's orchestral music to pupils with acute behavioural problems during science classes has enabled her to conduct normal lessons and achieve satisfactory academic results. Before, she says, 'the idea even of achieving silence in class was laughable.'

> Developing musical ability can help improve self-confidence, literacy and, some believe, enhance brain power

Sue Hallam of the Institute of Education is researching the effect of various kinds of music on children with and without behavioural problems. 'In one study, special-needs children were played music they themselves had selected as being "calm and relaxing" while they tackled maths exercises. The findings were that more and better maths was completed. A similar exercise in a mainstream primary school threw up comparable results.' Other fascinating research is suggesting to Hallam that varied styles of music – more or less 'aggressive' – can even affect the way children choose endings to stories when offered different moral alternatives.

Spotting potential

There remains the question of how to spot the child with the potential to develop rapidly. No problem, perhaps, for the parent who is a Friend of Covent Garden, takes holidays at the Edinburgh Festival and has been searching for signs of talent in his or her offspring since the first nappy-change. But even a parent with no particular musical background can notice the young child who is always singing and dancing, or maybe can't stop playing the piano, or loves listening to music. Hopefully staff at the child's school will also have spotted his or her ability, although standards of musical expertise available in schools have become increasingly variable. Most parents should have access to a local music centre, whether council-funded or independent. Look in the phone book under the local authority heading, or in *Yellow Pages* under 'music schools'. Specialist staff will hopefully be able to talk things through, make assessments and suggest courses of action. In the case of the very young, there may be a music kindergarten in your area – some of these, like the Monkey Music chain or Kodály-inspired groups (see Chapter 3) will have experienced, specialist staff on hand.

The country's specialist music schools and junior departments at the major conservatoires have wide experience of assessing talented children. Chetham's School of Music in Manchester, which has advertised its services with the phrase 'Is your child musical?', invites parents and children from across the country to apply for its individual assessment auditions. 'We conduct a range of non-pressurised aural tests,' says director of music Stephen Threlfall. 'We may get the child to sing back phrases played on the piano, clap rhythms, spot variations in the make-up of a chord and so on to find out just what ability the child has. The very least we can offer a parent is specialist advice on what to do next, what musical activities are available in their home area and so on.'

If your particular concern is for the benefit that music might bring to a child with special needs or disability, there are a number of organisations around Britain which can help with advice on therapy, tuition, courses and special events. The British Society for Music Therapy promotes the use of music in the treatment and education of children and adults suffering from emotional, physical and mental handicap. Sound Sense, based in Bury St Edmunds, provides advice on many aspects of making music fully available to those with disabilities. The Arts Council of England publishes a pack on the arts and disability and the *Music Education Yearbook* has many further contacts. *Andrew Green*

See back of book for contact details

DEALERS AND RESTORERS OF

INSTRUMENTS AND BOWS

OF THE

VIOLIN FAMILY

J.P. Guivier & Co. Ltd
(Est. 1863)

99 Mortimer Street
London W1N 7TA
Hours of opening: Mon-Fri: 9am-6pm
Sat: 10am-4pm
Main shop Tel: 0171-580 2560
Educational Dept: 0171-636 6499
Fax: 0171-436 1461

BEDALES AND DUNHURST SCHOOLS

(BOARDING & DAY 8-18)

"Recommended for bright and motived children of talent"
DAILY TELEGRAPH

Music Scholarships (up to half fees) with free instrumental tuition, are offered at 8+, 11+, 13+ and 16+. Additional funding available to those having proven need.

The principal instrument should be grade V (11+ and 13+) or VIII (16+).
Singing may be offered and composition work submitted in advance of audition.

**The tuition and achievement in Music at Bedales and Dunhurst are of an exceptionally high standard.
A large number of instrumental and choral groups flourish under the guidance of some 35 staff, five of whom are full time.**

Bedales is a co-educational full boarding school situated in the beautiful Hampshire countryside.

Further details from:

The Admissions Tutor, David Strutt
Bedales School, Steep, Petersfield, Hants. GU32 2DG
Tel: 01730 300100

Silent Series

The pinnacle of Yamaha's 100 year musical heritage: instruments you can't hear

This is no April Fool.   After years of making instruments the whole world wants to listen to, Yamaha's unique blend of craftsmanship and technology has created a range it doesn't have to.   **Silent Series** represents a new order in instrument development.   Practise in private, inside your headphones, where every musical nuance is faithfully reproduced.   And outside, barely a whisper, the world doesn't notice.   It's a giant leap for music kind, a blow against noise pollution..... buy one for your neighbours.

Yamaha Silent Violin   .   Yamaha Silent Piano   .   Yamaha Silent Brass   .   Yamaha DTX electronic drums

YAMAHA

2. Choosing an instrument

Falling in love or scientific selection?

SOME CHILDREN are musically monogamous. They fall truly, madly, deeply in love with the look and sound of one instrument in particular – at their first concert maybe. And that's it for life. In the majority of cases, however, the process of selecting a lasting partner may feel a little more like a blind date. But most music teachers and instrument dealers remain adamant that whatever gentle steering may take place, it's highly desirable that the final choice of instrument should rest with the person who intends playing it. As we shall see, circumstances may often narrow the options, but the principle should remain the same if at all possible. Children are more likely to stick with a partner they chat up themselves.

There have been attempts to apply detailed science to the process of selecting an instrument. You may find the odd book in your local library which suggests matching finger type, lip size, chest expansion and goodness knows what else to precise instruments. But another science – simple chemistry – is ultimately what should matter. 'For example, a child may not have ideal fingers for the piano,' says James Walker, head of the junior department at the Welsh College of Music and Drama, 'but if he or she is passionate about keyboard playing then the likelihood is that they're going to do well. What's sad is if the choice is an accident – maybe the school orchestra needs a bassoon, the teacher happens to find one in the back of a cupboard – that sort of thing. The ideal situation is one where the child is able to hear, see and touch the range of instruments before deciding. Here in Cardiff we run a series of discovery days open to any child. Staff demonstrate instruments, children are allowed to try them and there's a concert showing them

2

in action. It's important that parents are fully involved in the process.'

Mostyn Davies, head of the Cardiff County and Vale of Glamorgan Music Service, likes children to consider the implications of any choice of instrument. 'For example, they may be able to make quite a nice sound on the flute or clarinet straight away, compared to the scratchy noise you have to put up with for a while on the violin, but these days you're very likely to face huge competition to get into a school or youth orchestra – flutes and clarinets have grown enormously in popularity. So you could miss out on an experience which is important not just musically but also in terms of social and personal development. If a child is interested in the guitar or piano he or she might like to consider that they're quite solitary instruments; you tend to have far fewer opportunities for playing with groups and orchestras.'

But are you really going to settle on an instrument before discovering there's someone at school or elsewhere in your locality to teach it? A really exceptional teacher can be more important than the instrument you choose. 'Particularly on some of the less popular instruments, like cello and bassoon, you can never be sure until you take the trouble to find out,' says Richard Hickman of the Federation of Music Services. 'Sometimes a woodwind teacher, say, will be able to give the basic tuition on an instrument that isn't his or her speciality – but what happens as the child progresses? There's also the question of how you go about the business of hiring or buying an instrument. It's plain common sense to get the advice of the teacher, both on the specific makes of instruments and prices.

> Always consider the implications of your choice of instrument. The existence of a good teacher in your area may be crucial

Sizing up the issue

The age at which a child can tackle a particular instrument may depend on his or her physical development, but in recent years manufacturers have put a great deal of effort into devising versions of instruments that enable them to be played earlier than previously. There was a time when a child wanting to start very young would be offered the violin or cello on reduced sizes, keyboards or, of course, the recorder. The Lyons C clarinet, flutes with curved head joints to allow for shorter arms, the 'mini-bass' and the new fagottini as an early double bass and bassoon respectively are all bringing starting ages down well below ten as makers have realised the importance of catching children early.

Some teachers prefer pupils to have their second teeth before starting oboe and clarinet. Both guitar and a range of percussion instruments can sensibly be started around the age of eight, hand size being a factor

in each case. Small-sized guitars are readily available. Percussion instru
ments are expensive (though can be hired), but as long as the child has
access to decent instruments for lessons either at school or privately, he
or she can work at home with sticks and a 'practice pad' – inexpensive
and effective for basic technical skills.

Myths tend also to surround the appropriate ages at which a child can
take up a brass instrument – whether it's lip size, the arrival of second
teeth, lung capacity or whatever. But Adrian Parker of Phil Parker Ltd, a
specialist brass dealer, insists that you don't have to
wait anything like as long as is sometimes thought
to play many instruments. 'For example, being old
enough to have the puff is not the issue; vibrating a
column of air is all about technique, not being beefy.
Young teeth shouldn't be harmed unless the child is
practising far too much. Often the main issue is
whether an instrument is too heavy or too long to hold up for any
length of time. But, for example, there are pocket trumpets and cornets
which can be played by kids as young as four or five. Small versions of
tubas can be played at, say, eight. The reason why the horn is usually
started later is that it's tricky technically, but the child can start with the
tenor horn, which is lighter and easier to play.'

**There are now
versions of some
instruments that
are built to suit
early beginners**

If your three-year-old really does hanker to play something that's
impractical, there's always the humble recorder or ocarina as the gateway to plenty of transferable musical skills. These don't deserve their
Cinderella, 'starter' instrument image if taught well.

Getting started

A recurring theme in this handbook is the uncertainty as to whether any
given primary school will be able to offer particular musical opportunities. When financial decision-making was devolved upon individual
boards of school governors by the last Conservative government,
schools themselves were handed the decision as to the level of priority
music should have within yearly budgets. In a good few cases the
'umbrella' music service offered by local education authorities dis-
appeared. Independently run music services have sprung up to plug the
gap in many areas, for example in go-ahead Kent and Northampton-
shire, but in some parts of the country the collapse of music provision
has been disastrous. The result, where the provision of instruments is
concerned, is that availability often depends on the enthusiasm of
individual headteachers and school governors. In a few schools the
situation is better than ever before as new financial independence frees
staff to advance the place of music. The stock of instruments may be

extensive, possibly available free on loan for beginners. But the overall picture is decidedly patchy. If you're in doubt, tackle your headteacher on the subject. You may be referred to the local authority music adviser or music centre, where help should be available.

'The situation varies so much from area to area,' says Richard Hickman, 'that it's simply impossible to say that a child can be guaranteed to play the instrument of their choice if they cannot afford to buy or hire. Some schools and local music services have excellent 'instrument banks', but many don't. Some schools and music services can provide an instrument free – many can't. Steering a child towards an undersubscribed instrument can work if done without undue pressure.'

> **Before buying an instrument, always consult a teacher and find out about the price range**

If you decide you do wish to buy or hire an instrument, having consulted a teacher, of course, then it's worth taking time to select a specialist shop with an excellent choice, even if it means a bit of a journey. Have a clear idea in your mind what you're going to pay. Make sure the member of staff who serves you really knows his or her stuff – a good shop will employ at least some trained musicians. 'Parents often arrive without a clue about how they're going about things,' says Rachel Carpenter of the Herga Music store in Harrow. 'If they'd talked to a teacher or two they'd be far better equipped to make their choice.'

Most shops run some kind of hiring scheme, although it may not apply to every instrument. In many cases your child will expect, in due course, to be moving on to a larger-sized instrument, a fact that may well affect the decision over whether to hire or buy. Any shop with a track record of dealing regularly with young musicians is going to be realistic about the likelihood of a child abandoning his or her instrument in the early stages. The Music Centre in Tunbridge Wells, for example, runs a 'try-buy' scheme, whereby parents pay a deposit representing 20 per cent of the value of an instrument for a three-month trial period, after

ACTION POINTS

● It's best if the child can explore a range of instruments before choosing one – some colleges and music services hold open days

● Remember, if you choose a more popular instrument you may face stiff competition for entry to schools and orchestras

● Before making your choice, check there is a good specialist teacher in your area

● If your child is likely to move on to a larger instrument it is better to hire in the first instance. Most specialist shops run hire schemes

● When considering a second study, it's a good idea to choose the keyboard if you play an orchestral instrument and vice versa

which they can pay the balance or return the instrument and lose the deposit. Rushworth's in Liverpool gives an 80 per cent refund on the price of any instrument returned within six months. Customers who experiment with a cheap instrument from the same store can get their money back if they return to buy a more expensive model.

'Once the child has made the decision over what instrument to play I think it's up to the parents to make sure they keep at it,' says Chris Penfold of the Music Centre. 'Often they return an instrument saying they're sorry they let the child choose when it's really they who've been weak over practice. Parents also often make a point of choosing the cheapest instrument in a way that gives the child the clear message that they can give it up if they want to.' It's a view endorsed by James Walker at the Welsh College of Music and Drama. 'We ask parents to make sure that the child learns solidly for at least one year. During that time we continually assess the situation. If then it's felt things really aren't working then we consider moving them on to another instrument.'

Doubling up for the future

Musical monogamy is one thing, but there is also the entirely legitimate and laudable practice of instrumental two-timing. Some children may set their sights early on going to music college, where they will be expected to study a second instrument. Anticipating that requirement, junior departments of the main conservatoires and the country's specialist music schools ensure their pupils have a second string to their bow. Other children may simply be so musically keen (yes, it happens) that they want to explore other instruments just for fun. Passion may be the deciding factor in the choice, but stop and consider the implications of taking up one additional instrument rather than another.

Music colleges expect students to play a second instrument. The keyboard is a wise choice for a richer understanding of harmony

Janet Lasky of the junior department at Trinity College of Music in London offers some very straightforward advice. 'If you're already playing an orchestral instrument, I firmly advise taking up the keyboard. You learn to read two clefs, you get a richer understanding of harmony and the balance between treble and bass. Conversely, if you're a keyboard player, then choose an orchestral instrument and remember that orchestras are always crying out for bassoons, violas, horns and double basses. As a keyboard player you've probably missed out on ensemble playing and the social side of being in an orchestra.'

Many children will find they've changed a great deal physically by the time they come to choose a second instrument, which will increase the options open to them. 'Talented children from less well-off backgrounds can often find help with bursaries at conservatoires to enable them to acquire another instrument,' says Lasky. 'But don't start a second instrument until you know you can put in double the amount of practice time! That's vital.' *AG*

Stringed instruments: where to look at different stages

	Dealers	Violin shops	Auction houses	Antiques shops	Private collectors	Modern workshops
School learners		•				
Adult beginners		•			•	•
Music students & serious amateurs		•		•	•	•
Young professionals	•	•	·		•	•
Top professionals	•		•		•	•

Stringed instrument: guide prices

	Violin	Viola	Cello/Bass*
Small sizes	£60	£120	£220/£765*
School outfits Grade 1-5/6	£100-£600	£125-£725	£350+/£850+
Grade 8 & county youth orchestra	£800-£3,000	£900-£3,500	£2,000-£5,000
Adult beginners	£1,000+	£1,500+	£2,000+
Music students & serious amateurs	£1,500-£4,000	£1,750-£4,500	£2,000-£5,000
Young professionals	£4,000+	£4,500+	£5,000+
Top professionals	£10,000+	£12,000+	£15,000+

Bows and cases only included in first two categories. Add £250-£1,000+ for violin/viola bows, £750-£1,500+ for cello bows. *For a Korean bass. A Yorke mini-bass is the best-quality children's instrument, at £1,095/£1,150

Pianos: guide prices

	Upright	5'3" Baby grand	6' Grand
Basic (second-hand)	£650+	£2,000	£2,500
Basic (new)	£1,300-£2,000	£6,500	£10,000
Quality (second-hand)	£1,500+	£3,500+	£6,000-£10,000
Quality (new)	£2,250+	£7,500+	£13,000+

Wind instruments: guide prices

	Flute	Oboe	Clarinet	Bassoon	Alto /Ten Sax
Basic (second-hand)	£230	£500	£230	£1,800	£500/£575
Basic (new)	£320	£800	£320	£2,600	£600/£700
Mid (second-hand)	£750	£650	£450	£2,000	£750
Mid (new)	£1,000	£1,500	£600	£3,500	£1,000
Top (second-hand)	£1,800	£2,500	£850	£4,000	£1,500
Top (new)	£2,500+	£3,500+	£2,000+	£10,000+	£2,000+

Brass instruments: guide prices

	Trumpet	Trombone	Horn	Tuba
Beginner	£300 (new)	£400 (new)	£300 (s-h)	£800 (s-h)
Serious student	£1,500	£1,500	£4,000	£4,000

3. Finding a teacher

How to track down the key person

S OME SCIENTISTS now reckon the foundations of musical learning can be traced to the womb. It's certainly true that the weight of opinion among educationalists and researchers has swung behind the idea that early aural training – even from as young as a few months – is of immense benefit to child development.

Music kindergartens have sprung up all over the place. Before you commit to one, though, check out what sort of musical as well as pastoral training those in charge have. A good way to find such groups is to contact your local National Childbirth Trust branch, since most advertise through them. Some local music centres offer kindergartens run by qualified staff. Many will be independently-run, such as the London-based Monkey Music, for ages six months to four years. All such groups offer different games aimed at developing simple musical awareness, games which should become part of 'normal' home life in order to be really effective. It is important that you persist for at least a term: an eight-month-old may have the odd bad day, but if music is presented by the parent as a positive experience which everyone joins in, it will come to be seen as a natural activity.

Most good, imaginative teachers will draw on many different formal techniques of child music training, developing their own approach. These include the methods of Carl Orff and Zoltan Kodály. 'Kindermusik' groups base their ideas on the work of Orff, the German composer and music educationalist. The heart of his thinking was to encourage children to explore their own musical imaginations before an instrument is taught formally – learning to see music and speech alike as languages and musical activity as co-operative and social. The focus might, for example, be playing word games that highligh rhythm, or helping the child shape his or her own musical ideas in a improvisatory way, maybe in response to a picture.

The Kodály concept

One of the more prominent schools of pre-instrumental training is tha based on the ideas of the Hungarian composer Zoltán Kodály. Unti recently, those ideas made relatively little impact, but they are nov spreading steadily. Not every kindergarten teacher preaching his gospe may be fully trained by one of the national Kodály-inspired bodies – i could be worth checking. Both the British Kodály Academy and the Kodály Institute of Britain run three-year part-time courses to trair teachers with a certificate to prove it at the end. If in doubt, ask to see such evidence. Kodály principles lie behind a range of other training practices which are growing in popularity, notably Colourstrings, Colourkeys and Dalcroze Eurhythmics.

Kodály passionately believed that developing keen awareness o such basics as rhythm and pitch through singing was vital grounding fo long-term musical development. This aural training should precede the serious study of an instrument. 'Training the "inner ear" so that these basics become in-built remains the key aim,' says David Vinden of London's Trinity College of Music and director of courses for the British Kodály Academy. 'Kodály classes are increasingly available around the country. Children can start learning at the age of three in group sessions, which is good for social skills and keeps fees per parent very low. Musical games develop step-by-step awareness of high and low, loud and soft, fast and slow and many other facets of musicianship. Memorising is vital to the process.' Groups will normally be sized between six and 12.

> Kodály believed that learning basics such as rhythm and pitch through singing was vital for development

Around the age of five, children learn the hand-signal system that Kodály borrowed in the Twenties from the British choral educator John Curwen's innovation of teaching singing by the tonic 'sol-fa' method. 'Children are gradually enabled to sing musical intervals with great accuracy just by obeying the signals, relying on that inner ear,' says David Vinden. 'Repetition is at the heart of learning. What the child learns from all of this is then related to simple musical notation on a stave as the child moves towards playing an instrument.' Neither the British Kodály Academy nor the Kodály Institute of Britain currently publishes a register of teachers and kindergartens, although both respond to specific requests for information.

Finding a teacher

3

Dalcroze Eurhythmics (devised early in the century by Émil Jacques Dalcroze) adapts Kodály principles in terms of physical expression and is generally taught in conjunction with the Kodály singing approach. Movement is the Dalcroze way of internalising musical concepts. 'For example,' says Karin Greenhead, a leading Dalcroze exponent, 'you might ask a child to walk at one pace to a given rhythm, then walk twice as fast, then twice as fast again as a way of feeling the difference between quavers, crotchets and minims. Children can do complicated cross-rhythms in similar fashion. They can also express different types of musical phrasing in movement. It's all geared to giving the child an advantage when it comes to the next stage of their musical development, but Dalcroze can be useful to musicians at every stage of their lives.' Dalcroze teachers are trained for a minimum of two years part-time and the Dalcroze Society is legally entitled to proceed against those who use the brand name without the requisite training.

> The Dalcroze method teaches children phrasing, rhythm and beat by making them express it in movement

Colourstrings/Colourkeys has the same Kodály-inspired starting point. It then takes the pupil on into instrumental tuition. The prime mover here was the Hungarian-born violinist Géza Szilvay, whose work in Finland with children of all abilities has won huge international praise, not least through the virtuosity of his Helsinki Junior Strings. 'After the early Colourstrings training,' says Pat Wislocki of the Szilvay Foundation, 'children will choose an instrument at the age of five from violin, cello, piano, mini-bass [miniature double bass] and guitar. The children are encouraged to think of strings or keys as being coloured to stimulate their imaginations. All the time the emphasis is on singing and playing, on playing the way you learned to sing. And if you can sing in tune you play in tune.' Teachers at kindergarten level offering Colourstrings should have received training at one of the organisation's courses run throughout the year. These have been recognised by Trinity College of Music in London. Colourstrings runs a helpline for parents wishing to know about the local availability of teachers.

If you don't introduce your child to any of the Kodály-based experiences at kindergarten level, you may still like to consider a Kodály-trained instrumental teacher if you opt for private tuition. They can be found in many areas of music teaching including in schools, but you may need help from one of the organisations mentioned above. If you're unsure if this is for your child, go along to a Kodály/Colourstrings/Dalcroze session. Even if you choose a more mainstream teacher, any Kodály-based training is likely to continue reaping benefits in terms of general musicianship.

Introducing Suzuki

The principle that very young children receive the most soli
foundation by learning aurally rather than moving too swiftly int
reading music also applies to one of the 'buzz' instrumental teachin
methods of the Seventies and Eighties – 'Suzuki'. Thi
Just as children was pioneered by the Japanese guru Shin'ich
don't learn to Suzuki, who died only recently at the age of 9ᶜ
read before they Suzuki teaching in violin, piano, cello, flute an
speak, Suzuki guitar is well-established – more instruments will fol
pupils don't learn low. You can start as young as two-and-a-half. Som
to read music musicians snipe at the Suzuki method, suggesting i
until they can play churns out performing automata, but enthusiast
with confidence claim it is starting to show its worth in the UK as stu
dents begin to take up places in major orchestras.

The essence of the Suzuki method, says Birte Kelly of the Britisl
Suzuki Institute, is that children 'learn to play in the same way as the
learn to speak – by listening and imitating. Just as children don't learn t
read before they can speak, so Suzuki pupils don't learn to read musi
until they're playing confidently. Any child can be taught by thi
method, which has been successful partly because of the emphasis we
place on the parents being very much part of the process. Children learr
to memorise tunes by listening to them on CD or cassette at home. Ir
lessons they learn how to play those same tunes by copying the
demonstration given in small chunks by their teacher. Making it fun anc
praising the pupil for every step taken are watchwords among Suzuk
teachers. Parents are expected to be present, taking notes and receiving
instruction on how practice at home is to be organised and encouraged
– even learning an instrument themselves.

Suzuki teaching has been criticised on the grounds that the lack of
emphasis on reading music in the early stages excludes children from
playing in ensembles, but Birte Kelly insists that this problem has been
fully addressed in recent years. 'We now teach "pre-reading skills"
before the age of five, with reading music being gradually introduced at
around the age of five itself. By the time children are seven or eight,
they're probably reading as well as any of their peers, although there
may be the tendency to continue playing by ear after all the training of
the memory. I think some of the criticism of the past arose because
Suzuki children were pushed into playing in orchestras early simply
because they had such good basic skills.'

Birte Kelly urges parents in doubt about the qualifications of any
teacher advertising the Suzuki method to get in touch with the British
Suzuki Institute for advice. 'If such a teacher has no other musical

qualifications then there could be real problems.' The Institute runs ts own minimum two-year part-time course. It also trains, to strict standards, musicians with no college background to teach the method.

Is there a teacher at school?

All such named methods nonetheless represent no more than a relatively small part of the totality of music training and tuition available in this country. Searching out any of the above options may be difficult in a given area and, for many parents, turning to the primary or middle school for instrumental tuition may be the most convenient and financially viable option. But the same problems that are dogging the provision of instruments in many schools are also affecting the availability of teachers. On the one hand, class teaching of basic musical awareness is generally deemed to have improved since the introduction of national curricula in the various parts of the United Kingdom – notwithstanding the fact that the Labour government has recently deemed music a non-compulsory subject at Primary level. Instrumental tuition, however, is in crisis at primary and middle school level in many areas and localities. *Making Music*, a report published in 1997 by the Associated Board of the Royal Schools of Music, paints a worrying picture. Based on research carried out in England, Scotland and Wales, *Making Music* suggests the numbers of children aged five to 14 playing musical instruments declined from 45 per cent to 41 per cent between 1993 and 1996 – a fall especially acute among boys. The entire decline took place among children aged between five and ten, especially children from families in social grades C1 and C2.

A more recent survey of 692 UK primary schools conducted for the *Times Educational Supplement*, published in April this year, presents a still more worrying picture, both in terms of the outlook for music teaching in the curriculum and instrumental tuition in schools, which is seen increasingly as the preserve of children whose parents can afford to pay. Access to free tuition varies widely across Britain, English schools being bottom of the league table with only one in five pupils benefiting, although subsidies available to parents often compensate.

Now that schools control their own budgets music provision depends on the priorities of the Governors

Most commentators blame the decline in instrumental playing on measures introduced by the last Conservative government and continued under Labour to grant schools the power to run their own budgets. This has, in many areas, sounded the death knell for the system whereby local education authorities funded support systems of music teachers available to teach in schools, run youth orchestras and so on. Often the existence of a strong local teaching provision is now in the hands of independent music services. But there is no uniform standard of provision across the country.

'The picture is extremely variable,' says John Coe, information officer of the National Association for Primary Education.

Parents who can pay for individual tuition are often expected to do so; some schools offer it in the same way as free school meals

'Now that schools are in charge of their own budgets, everything may depend on the skills possessed by full-time staff and on what money can be allocated by governors to bring in specialist music teachers from outside. You may or may not have to pay for instrumental tuition. Each school has to publish a prospectus, so if you're a parent considering where to send your child you should be able to get an idea of which schools are best for music in your area.'

'There never was a golden age as far as music tuition in schools was concerned,' says Richard Hickman of the Federation of Music Services, 'but prior to the devolution of budgeting to individual schools parents were certainly much more likely to find that at least group instrumental tuition was provided free. Now schools are allowed to charge fees up to a maximum of four children in a group. These days it's very often the case that parents who can pay are expected to do that – especially for individual tuition. Where parents can't afford to pay, some schools offer free tuition in the same way that free school meals are provided. If, as a parent, you're uncertain about what music is on offer, approach the headteacher, even if you think the school doesn't have a strong emphasis on music. At the very least he or she will pass you on to the local education authority music advisor/inspector, and with a bit of luck there will be a music support service which can offer lessons outside school hours. It just isn't possible to guarantee that a particular school will be able to offer a specialist teacher on the less popular instruments – a local music centre may be the answer.'

Vetting your teacher

If you decide to pay for private tuition, it's worth taking just the sort of care with your choice of teacher as you would (hopefully) employ in selecting a doctor or a solicitor. 'Private music teaching is in many ways an unregulated profession,' says Heli Ignatius Fleet, an executive committee member of the European Piano Teachers' Association (EPTA) in the UK. 'In Britain there are no agreed qualifications – anyone can set themselves up. A poor teacher can do plenty of damage at the important early stages. Is music clearly being presented to the child as an enriching experience rather than just a matter of playing the right notes? Are bad habits, like poor posture, being tackled? Is the child anxious or does he or she look forward to the next lesson? Does the teacher push pupils through exams just for the sake of it? As a parent I would insist on a consultation lesson to assess the rapport between child and teacher. There's no hard and fast rule about having a male teacher for a boy or a female for a girl – it's far more a matter of the teacher's expertise first and then the personal chemistry. Good teachers show that they know they're accountable to you – they won't be defensive when it comes to talking about the pupil and what goes on in lessons.' EPTA recommends that parents should expect teachers to draw up a written contract specifying such items as the number of lessons per term and their length, the fees involved, the period of notice required for terminating lessons.

Michael Skinner of the National Association of Percussion Teachers (NAPTA) says even a non-musical parent can ask blunt, basic questions of a prospective teacher. 'You have every right to suss out the person you're paying for. You're entitled to ask them what qualifications they have. Do they have a teaching diploma? Find out more about their experience as teachers – what have their pupils achieved? Do they have a track record as a performer. Do they seem to enjoy their teaching?'

NAPTA and EPTA are two from a number of organisations representing teachers in given instrumental categories. ESTA, the European String Teachers Association, is another. Such organisations will embrace teachers favouring many different methods and systems of teaching. String teachers, for example, may subscribe to such methods as the Kato Havas (where the emphasis is on tackling tension and anxiety in playing). It can be confusing, so don't be frightened of asking basic questions of prospective teachers until you're satisfied. But just because a given teacher doesn't advertise – as most don't – a fancy-sounding method, it hardly need define them as stick-in-the-mud.

Check the teacher is presenting music as an enriching experience, not just a matter of technique

Those who apply to become members of professional organisations may or may not be strictly vetted in respect of their teaching abilities, although the fact that they have taken the trouble and paid their money to join such a body says something about their outlook. But take reasonable care when selecting names from any published lists of teachers or the information from your local library. The Musicians Union publishes a *National Directory of Instrumental Teachers*, available in music shops or direct from the MU. If you want help seeing the wood for the trees, both the Incorporated Society of Musicians and EPTA (UK) publish no-nonsense sheets of 'things to look for' in a teacher which can apply to any instrument. EPTA suggests that teachers should be seen, for example, to 'develop memory and improvising skills', 'introduce a variety of musical styles' and 'report regularly to parents on pupils' progress'

The register of teachers available from the Incorporated Society of Musicians is carefully regulated. 'Anyone listed has to have been vouched for by two existing ISM members and to have satisfied our private teacher committee about their training and experience,' says the organisation's chief executive Neil Hoyle. 'On fees, our recommended rate is £16 per hour for individual lessons.'

The need for specialist training courses for instrumental teachers is now increasingly being addressed in part-time courses offered by, for example, Trinity College of Music and the Guildhall School of Music, as well as by the Associated Board of the Royal Schools of Music. As yet their influence may be limited countrywide, but John Stephens, head of music education at Trinity College, says it's vital that 'there should be ways in which instrumental teachers are both kept up to date with the most recent thinking on teaching methods and encouraged to keep their own skills going as performers.'

Finally, what about the touchy subject of exams (see Chapter 5)? Are they necessary? Should a prospective teacher's attitude influence your choice? Very possibly so, says Heli Ignatius Fleet. 'On the one hand, exams will remain the system by which standards are measured. But they may not be the only appropriate goal. Ask if the teacher concerned is keen to work towards exams. If they are, ask what the plan is. Preparing for exams should be seen as a periodic departure from the broader, more general work on the repertoire – not the other way around. Exams mean a narrow repertoire focus, and can lead to an emphasis on very cautious, correct playing. While working for an exam a pupil can feel that anything he or she does is being assessed. It's certainly important that there's something to work towards, but that might mean a concert arranged privately by the teacher, or perhaps taking part in a local festival.' *AG*

ACTION POINTS

● Early music training uses games and songs to awaken the inner ear.

● Always have a trial lesson before committing

● Make sure you find out what a teacher's qualifications are

● Find out if their attitude to exams is rigid or flexible

● You pay for what you get: does this teacher's rates match up with the ISM recommended rates?

● Look at teacher societies lists and the ISM register

See back of book for contact details

4. Helping with practice

How to conquer the dreaded 'P' word

THIS IS THE CHAPTER you've been waiting for: how to convince your child that regular visits to the practice room will do no lasting damage to his or her health and may just bring about a sense of what you could fancifully call 'pleasure through progress'.

Practice and progress go hand-in-hand. It's as true of music as it is of learning to drive a car, brewing home-made beer or perfecting a drop volley. As you may have read earlier (Chapter 1), researchers these days are tending to tone down the idea of natural musical talent, emphasising the role that simple hard work plays in producing excellence. It's harder now to blame lack of progress simply on lack of aptitude. There are, of course, well-motivated children who find practice fun and happily toddle off to get started on their own, but they're in a tiny minority. For many others, the likelihood is that lack of practice sets up a vicious circle in which the teacher's disappointment at results, even if expressed sensitively, produces resentment in the child, leading to increased reluctance to practise, rows with parents and so on, until music is associated simply with ill-feeling.

What teachers agree on – and here's the crunch – is that parents have a vital role to play in practice, whether they are themselves musical or not. Some modern teaching methods such as Suzuki demand that the parent learns and practises with the child. Far less easy for the child to squirm out of practice, but demanding a heavy commitment from the parent. Even when the teaching methods are more traditional, a child starting very young will need plenty of guidance and support during practice, which is almost bound to require that the parent attends at least some lessons at the start to understand what needs working at.

The purpose of practising is to achieve some simple, short-term goals before the next lesson, ones which the child has agreed on and are easy enough to remember. These tasks should be chosen according to the individual's aural and technical ability, otherwise they will be demoralising. If it gets to the stage where the child has no idea why he or she is continuing to practise a piece, then there needs to be a conversation between the teacher, pupil and parent to explain why.

Avoiding warfare

The potential for fights over practice increases as the child grows older. 'The problem,' says violin teacher Kate Clarke, 'is that children's out-of-school time is so easily swallowed up by so many leisure activities and distractions. It needs an adult to ensure that practice has a place in the schedule. But a lot of mothers and fathers seem happy to send their children to lessons without supervising practice at all.'

The parent, Clarke advises, needs to agree with the child a regular time to practise, provide a quiet space and then hold to that. 'An eye needs to be kept on what the teacher has asked the child to work on,' she says. 'Usually there will be a book in which the details are written down and some teachers will ask the parent to sign it. Always the parent needs to offer encouragement. There's no hard and fast rule. If you do sit in the room you shouldn't try to be the teacher, but you can help the child to organise their time. Always encourage!'

There are several aspects of playing that a parent can helpfully monitor: their physical relationship to the instrument (ensure you know what the correct posture is); preventing over-hurried practice and the habit of confused, inconsistent bowing/fingering (depending on the instrument) and ensuring that the rhythm is kept steady. Says piano teacher Julia Freeman, 'Playing pieces at a moderate speed but with a steady beat produces organised playing, which the teacher can then move forward musically and technically.' One way of controlling the beat during practice is for the teacher to give a specific metronome mark for the week's work, ie one that is slower than the given speed.

Learn the correct posture your child should have when playing and listen out for a steady rhythm

Another way children can be encouraged is to suggest revisiting easier pieces they can already play well, and let them perform them for friends or family. Says Julia Freeman, 'Talk about the piece they are playing and how it sounds. Bring the subject of musical character into general conversation. Children like to feel their ideas and skills are observed and valued and they all like to show off safely! Channel this.'

Repetition is a necessary evil of practice, but it can be made less edious by playing the phrase with a different speed, volume, touch or expressive character. Piano teacher and author Diana Tickell has written imaginatively on how to keep the process of practising free of drudgery in her *Pocket Practice Book* (see back of book for details), but she remains uncompromising when it comes to the need for a basic daily routine of playing. 'Regularity of practice is so vital. Parents only store up trouble for themselves if this isn't accepted, with the child always feeling mum or dad will cave in and make exceptions to the rule if they argue long enough. It's much the best thing if a child plays for ten minutes a day rather than doing a big practice once a week. Practice needs to become as normal as brushing the teeth. You can give the child as much choice as possible – over the room they feel most comfortable practising in, maybe, or what regular time of day it's going to happen – but children can't have a total-ly free choice when it comes to the need to practice. If they don't perse-vere, it may be that they have little choice about whether they can play an instrument later in life and come to regret that.'

> **Most children won't go near music college, but that doesn't mean they can't derive great pleasure from making music**

However, Tickell suggests that as well as assessing their own role in supervising practice, parents need to look closely at how the teacher handles the whole thorny subject. 'Traditionally I don't think that music colleges have given enough status to teaching as a first-class option for the people they train. Many musicians then drift into teaching feeling like second-class citizens, only really able to relate to the idea of excel-lence and the rigid discipline and technique that goes into producing that. This is certainly the case with a good few musicians who've written on the subject of practice. Teachers are then confronted with a situation where the vast majority of their pupils are in varying degrees far less dedicated than that. Most won't be going anywhere near music college. But that doesn't mean they can't learn to achieve enormous satisfaction from making music. So it's vital that teachers don't lose sight of the sense of enjoyment which such children need. Instead, what you get whenever teachers meet are groans round the table about how their pupils don't practise.'

Tickell insists that the child shouldn't feel he or she is being pressurised into something. 'If a child clearly isn't enjoying what he or she is being asked to do in practice and it really is getting in the way of progress, well, what can he or she enjoy playing? For example, if that happens to be melodies from pop songs, that's fine. If it's what's neces-sary to stimulate the child to play with enjoyment, that's no problem. I feel strongly that we must get away from the distinction between playing and practice – it's all playing. While children are playing they're all the time becoming more familiar with the instrument. I feel it's so important that the teacher recognises that and offers praise. If they don' – and there will be those teachers who disagree with this approach – talk it through. It's not saying that playing classical repertoire and work-ing on technique will stop. What's needed is a strategy for the individ-ual child and that's going to require communication between parent and teacher.' Julia Freeman agrees that playing of pop tunes can be fun but warns that it is unlikely to cure a complete loss of interest. Pop pieces seem attractive because they are less challenging technically and expressively, and do not develop sound in the same way. 'The child who won't stick at a classical piece will rarely perfect their performance of a pop piece either.'

Star percussionist Evelyn Glennie agrees that the idea of practice needs redefinition, suggesting that parents discuss with teachers 'the role which experimenting and improvising with sound can play. It can be such an exciting way to open up new areas of highly personal enjoy-ment. Children need at times to get away from the printed page, the scales and arpeggios. I love to see youngsters using their instrument to create their own pictures of rain, trees, birds – whatever it may be, and having the freedom to depart at times from "correct" technique.'

Another way to spice up practice can be to encourage plenty of sight-reading, the child choosing what to play. In the short-term, a swift turnover of pieces helps prevent boredom creeping in, as it can do when the child only works at perfect-ing pieces. In the longer-term, sight-reading is a skill that can open up a world of collaboration with others in adult life, in chamber music playing as well as orchestras.

Michael Hambourg, music coun-sellor for the National Association for Gifted Children, says 'unorthodox' practice regimes may be all the more important for children with particular ability. 'They can display acute signs of boredom and may appear to achieve little. But very often the ones I see are in fact highly creative children, with very original, indepen-

ACTION POINTS

● Check for rushing, rhythmic control, posture and inconsistent fingering/bowing

● Set a regular practice time, make sure there is quiet space and see your child sticks to it

● Ten minutes a day is better than a long session once a week

● Playing should be fun. If your child is becoming demotivated try going back to an earlier piece they have already mastered

● Encourage plenty of sight-reading with the child choosing what to play

● Children usually reject fussing, drilling, fiddling – just let them get on with it!

dent minds. For them, highly structured lessons and practice sessions may be the cause of their frustration. In fact, their creativity needs to be respected, if necessary, by changing to a teacher with more insight. Parents may find it more difficult to help with practice in such cases, but there are in fact plenty of ways in which they can reinforce creativity.'

Over-anxious, older children also need careful monitoring. Some children practise so much they stop listening to themselves, especially before an exam or an important performance. One way of 'standing back' is for them to tape themselves playing. Nothing escapes the objective ear of the microphone and a child can sometimes accept they are repeating a problem better from a machine than from a teacher or parent. Bad habits in posture may also creep in during intensive practice so it is a good idea to have a mirror in the room to check.

Whatever the methods and mechanics of helping a child with practice, it's a pretty narrow experience if it remains isolated. Anything that relates the rigours of the practice room to the wider world of music will help make sense of what the effort is all about. So many musical experiences can count as 'practice' in the broader sense of enhancing the child's appreciation, from attending quality concerts (look out for youth discount schemes) and listening to CDs or the radio, to exploring the ever-growing range of musical CD-ROMs (many public libraries now have CD-ROM facilities available either free or for a small payment). Actively invite your child's opinions about anything to do with music – including pop. It may need the wisdom of Solomon to find the best balance between stick and carrot, but one day they may be grateful you tried. *AG*

5. Exams and competitions

Public performance is all part of learning

ONCE A CHILD has mastered the very basics of the instrument they've chosen, it is likely that their teacher will start suggesting 'doing a grade', although if your child is very young this may be off-putting. The graded system, which began more than a century ago, still has a strong grip on practical music teaching in the UK. It is perfectly possible to learn an instrument to the highest standard without ever taking an exam. However, music isn't just about studying technique and plodding through increasingly demanding pieces; performing a piece that's been carefully prepared to the best of the child's ability is all part of music-making. Exams are one way of giving a pupil this opportunity; for the same reasons, many teachers also encourage pupils to take part in local competitive and non-competitive festivals.

Usually parents are surprised by their children's enthusiasm for music exams – children love collecting certificates. Check out the teacher's attitude; a good teacher will not push exams or competitions on a reluctant pupil. And if your child is absolutely adamant that he or she doesn't want to do them, that doesn't mean giving up music.

The best-known examining body in the UK is the Associated Board of the Royal Schools of Music. The other national examining boards are Trinity, the Guildhall, and the London College of Music. They each offer preparatory exams, then a series of grades rising from 1 to 8. If your child is having lessons at school, there may also be a system of grading devised locally; this may not even involve an exam as such – grades may be awarded as the pupil achieves objectives, such as performing a piece of a certain standard in school assembly. Teachers should explain which system is being used and specific requirements.

Preparing for exams

Exams normally consist of several parts: prepared pieces (usually three), scales and arpeggios, aural, sight-reading and sometimes general musicianship, or answering questions about the pieces played. Encouraging regular practice is vital (see Chapter 4). Neglecting it all week then doing an hour's work the night before the lesson is of little use; neither is playing through pieces and scales as quickly as possible once a day. Help your child to draw up a realistic practice timetable to prepare for the exam, working on just one or two pieces and a

Help your child draw up a realistic timetable for the exam, working on just one or two pieces and a few scales each session

few scales each session. Letting them tick it off or fill it in with stickers is often popular with younger children. Many object strongly to parents standing over them while they practise; on the other hand your support is invaluable even if you have no musical training. Suggest that they concentrate on the bars they find hardest, then play the piece as a whole to you at the end of the practice session. Scales and

arpeggios (which must be learned from memory) will be asked in a random order in the exam, so devise a 'practice pot' – write each key on separate pieces of paper (scales and arpeggios also separate), fold each piece up and put it in a pot. Let your child pick a few out at random; this

helps them learn to switch keys, or start with arpeggios as in an exam. Keen parents may wish to help their children master the aural tests; there are various coaching books and cassettes on the market, but check carefully with your child's teacher that they conform to the latest syllabus requirements of the correct exam board: be warned, there have been changes in recent years. However bored you are becoming with the pieces, try not to let it show and persuade your child to play to as many family and friends as you can – children only develop performing skills (and discover weak points) in such situations, so if the day of the exam is the first time they've played to an outsider, it's too late.

Don't overstress a young child by

ACTION POINTS

● A good teacher will not push exams or competitions on a reluctant child

● The real value of exams and festivals is the preparation and experience of performing which helps build confidence

● Write each scale and arpeggio on a bit of paper and put it in a 'practice pot' for your child to draw out at random

● There may be a local grading system which awards pupils grades for achieving objectives without exams

● Festivals give children a competitive chance to perform before an audience with a professional adjudicator

talking too much about the exam or your expectations. Explain that he or she will go into a room with the accompanist (unless they play piano or guitar) and be greeted by the examiner; occasionally there may be a moderator sitting in on the exam too. Examiners are trained to put candidates at their ease (admittedly some are better at this than others); in the main they will give little reaction to the performance, but will be making notes on a mark sheet during the exam. Usually the youngest candidates are the least nervous; nerves grow with age and are quite normal. A child who is well-prepared and used to performing to others will do best; encouraging slow, deep breathing, as well as adopting a philosophical attitude all help to overcome butterflies.

5

Seeking the spotlight

A child who is entering a local festival or competition may only need to prepare for one piece; however this should be as meticulously practised as for an exam. While festivals often have a competitive element, these days the emphasis is on giving entrants the chance to perform before an audience with the benefit of a professional adjudicator to provide comments to aid future development. Each festival will have its own flavour, so attending as a spectator is the best way of discovering what is required. Festivals have a strong social element and mingling with budding musicians of a similar age and standard, listening to them as well as being listened to, are all vital elements in confidence-building and developing performance skills for your child.

> Each festival has its own flavour. The best way of judging the standard is to go along as a spectator

Festivals may not like to stress the winner/loser element, but if your child has taken an exam he or she may pass, receive a merit or distinction, or sadly, fail. No parent could fail to feel a glow of pride when their child achieves a distinction, but if you come to expect the highest marks you may end up pressuring your child unduly; most children are pleased enough to have passed. Examiners and adjudicators, who are all experienced and highly trained musicians, are as objective as possible, but invariably candidates occasionally do less well, or even somewhat better than expected. Remember, only the Guildhall offers examiners who specialise in the instrument, as well as devising a unique marking system which considers specific aspects of the candidate's playing, with the aim of offering candidates and their teachers an expert assessment tailored to the instrument being examined. But at the end of the day, a good result is a great morale-booster – bad marks, naturally, tend to be put down to a grumpy examiner. Often criticism may help reinforce a point a teacher has been attempting to address for months and most children face a bad result with renewed determination to prove they can do better next time.

As a child progresses up the ladder towards Grade 8, be warned that Grade 5 theory or equivalent may be required before the later exams can be entered. Find out whether additional lessons to prepare for this will be needed. And while passing Grade 8 is in itself a great achievement, it's only the beginning of the training to become a professional musician: this is the absolute minimum standard required to be considered for music college. For more advanced students who want to be kept on their toes, the Associated Board also offers a Performance Assessment for those over the age of 16; candidates are invited to perform a 15-minute programme for a specialist examiner, whose comments are offered there and then. There is no pass or fail; it is open to any standard and is also suitable for those unable to cope with standard exam requirements. Sometimes it is considered a sort of 'Grade 9' for candidates who are considering whether or not to go to music college. They will have the benefit of advice from an expert on their instrument (often a professor at one of the colleges) who is used to hearing students on a higher level.

The real value of any exam or festival has been in the preparation and experience of performing on the day; a child who learns to handle the situation with confidence will be developing useful skills for later in life. But there is plenty more to music-making – exams or festivals should never form the be-all and end-all of your child's musical education. *Elestr Lee*

See back of book for contact details

6. Ensembles and orchestras

Making more friends through music

FOR TENS OF THOUSANDS of children across Britain, Saturday morning – and often afternoon as well – means 'orchestra'. Or maybe 'band', 'quartet', 'jazz combo' or 'youth choir'. Locally based music centres, whether attached to local education authorities, or independent, come fully to life at a time when many of us are interested only in a lie-in. Very often they are located in schools. On offer generally is a range of rehearsal-based ensemble activity in which the players are graded by ability and trained by specialists.

A good teacher will know both where your nearest centre is located and also when is an appropriate moment to put a child forward. Some centres take children a matter of weeks after they've started to play, others may require roughly Grade 2 or 3 standard of playing with the basics in place. 'There's some tremendous material published for beginners to play,' says Helen Blakeman, head of music services for Buckinghamshire. 'The sound such children make may be rather hard on the ear, but the chance to play in an ensemble of any standard offers so much. Above all it does wonders in developing concentration. You have to keep to your own part without being distracted, listen to what's going on around, watch the beat and so on.'

The aim at most centres is to provide children with stepping stones from ensemble to ensemble through gradually ascending levels of competence, hopefully to county youth orchestra/band level. Paul McCrisken, senior instrumental tutor for the music service of the North-Eastern Education and Library Board in Ballymena, Northern Ireland, believes Saturday morning orchestras can be a vital element in holding children's musical interest. 'Our experience is that a child who plays in one of our ensembles, whether a band or an orchestra, is less likely to give up his or her instrument. There are always concerts to aim for, providing a focus for the rehearsals. There are some children who find it very difficult to practise their instrument at home – quite apart from their natural reluctance, the parents may be unsympathetic to music and may not help by providing the child with space and quiet. So without ignoring the importance of daily practice, in these situations Saturday mornings may provide the main opportunity to become more familiar with the instrument between lessons.'

According to John Ellis, head of the County Durham music service, 'children who take individual lessons at school are often the subject of jokes for carrying a violin or oboe case, but on Saturday mornings they mix with other musical children and realise they're not alone or strange. They gain more technical confidence because they're **Saturday orchestra** not playing on their own and they learn from each **gives musical** other's mistakes. There will generally be a range of **children the** music to play that embraces popular music and jazz **chance to socialise** (see Chapter 11) as well as classical pieces.' **with other** Costs to the parent are kept as low as possible and **musicians and** music centres will generally make provision for those **learn from them** on income support. Buckinghamshire, for example, charges £36 per term for a child to play in up to two bands, a supplement of £8 being added for each additional ensemble for the really keen. Other music centres charge ensemble by ensemble.

County youth orchestras

Most county youth orchestras require a minimum of Grade 5 on an instrument and the competition can be tough, depending on what instrument you play. For the national orchestras, such as the National Youth Orchestra of Great Britain, the minimum entry requirement is Grade 8 with distinction and the competition for places requires the personality to cope with potentially nerve-racking auditions. That, however, is the top of the tree; entering and playing in junior orchestras needn't be anything like as scary. Depending on the county in which you live, there can be up to four other 'feeder' orchestras. Entry to these is usually by audition and the teacher will normally recommend that a child auditions when they feel the time is right.

Before signing up to a county youth orchestra, it's worth considering how they operate. Some youth orchestras rehearse weekly, such as the Hull Junior Philharmonic Orchestra and the Southampton Youth Orchestra and some work via intensive courses during the school holidays, such as the Bedfordshire County Youth Orchestra and the

Edinburgh Youth Orchestra. Others rehearse via a combination of both. In all cases there are pros and cons and it is important that the working environment suits your child. Weekly rehearsals are good for maintaining enthusiasm and for building friendships over a sustained period of time. But remember that this is quite a commitment.

Intensive courses in the school holidays mean there is something to look forward to and keep your child stimulated at a time when music lessons usually stop altogether. 'They are good for focusing a young person's mind on getting something done over a definite period of time,' says Michael Rose, conductor of the Bedfordshire County Youth Orchestra. 'There's the internal pressure to work as a team. Any one person could wreck the whole and that teaches a sense of responsibility very effectively.'

> Weekly rehearsals help maintain enthusiasm and foster friendships, but can be a big commitment for parent and child

6

Holiday courses are also good socially and culturally, particularly if the orchestra goes on tour abroad. But the intensive nature of such a working environment brings its own pressures, which may not suit every child. They may also disrupt family plans and cause tension if other children in the family are not involved in similar activities. These courses can be expensive, although there may be bursaries available through the county music service; ring your local county music service for information.

In all of the above cases one of the key factors in getting into any orchestra could be which instrument your child plays (see Chapter 2). It is nearly always the case that competition for entry to youth orchestras is very high for violins, cellos, and the main wind and brass instruments. It's possible that in choosing to play the double-bass, viola, horn, bassoon or percussion, your child may find entry in to a really good local or national orchestra much easier.

For information on many of the youth orchestras nationwide, contact the National Association of Youth Orchestras which provides information, not only on many of the orchestras, brass and wind bands, but also on events, awards, competitions and insurance.

Once hooked on the orchestral experience, your child may consider that this is what he or she wants to do as a career, in which case there are several orchestras catering for advanced students and young professionals: the Britten-Pears Orchestra and Baroque Orchestra, the London Philharmonic Youth Orchestra, the Young Musicians Symphony Orchestra and the European Union Youth Orchestra. Take your child to a concert – much more inspiring than reading glossy brochures!

In addition to the county and national youth orchestras, there are a number of specialist orchestras. These include the Jewish Youth Orchestra of Great Britain, the Methodist Association of Youth Clubs Orchestra and the National Youth Music Theatre Orchestra. The requirements vary, but entry is usually by audition. If your child's musical inclination lies beyond the classical orchestral repertoire, then it is worth looking into other local and national performing groups. There are brass and wind bands all over the country, and there is the National Youth Jazz Orchestra of Great Britain, and, in Scotland, the NYJO of Scotland and the Fife Youth Jazz Orchestra.

Saturdays at the conservatoire

Saturday is also a busy – and noisy – day at the major British music conservatoires. As the regular students sleep off their Friday nights, the colleges are invaded by members of their junior departments, some of them travelling hundreds of miles for a day of specialist tuition. Competition is fierce for places in such departments, although the Birmingham Conservatoire and the Royal Northern College of Music currently run projects to encourage string playing which admit each and every applicant for tuition from the age of three and six respectively. 'String instruments are simply not being taught the way they were – there's been a huge drift to woodwind,' says Heather Slade-Lipkin, head of the junior school at the Birmingham Conservatoire. 'It's very worrying for the future.'

The Welsh College of Music and Drama, the Royal Academy of Music and the Guildhall School of Music and Drama run pre-junior departments, starting as early as age four. Normally, entry to junior departments is by audition and some colleges will see potential juniors at any time during the year. A rough standard of expectation is that applicants should have at least a good pass at Grade 4 or 5 on their main instrument by the age of 11, although many enter at this standard well before that age. But less specifically, junior departments say they are looking for outstanding potential. 'It's not simply a matter of looking at the

ACTION POINTS

● Local music centres offer lively ensemble activity on Saturdays with players graded by ability

● The aim is to provide stepping stones to county youth orchestra/band level and the experience can often enthuse a child who dislikes home practice

● The major conservatoires have junior departments offering Saturday tuition

● Entry is by audition and applicants should have at least a good Grade 4 pass

● Competition for county youth orchestras is fierce but many counties have 'feeder' orchestras

Grade certificate,' says Jonathan Willcocks, director of the junior department at the Royal Academy of Music in London. 'Auditions are as user-friendly as we can make them – it's so important we hear children at their best. We encourage parents to bring their children to our open day so they know a little about us in advance. The audition itself is informal. No one wears a suit, everything is on Christian name terms and no more than two assessors are in the room at the same time. It's also vital we find out how much it's the child who wants to come and how much the pushy parent.'

Most students successful in passing the audition will be offer a county scholarship or bursary. Fees for the junior departments range from around £400 to over £600 per annum, less for the pre-juniors. Cash to subsidise individual fees, where necessary, comes variously from local authorities, county scholarships and the colleges' own scholarships and means-tested bursaries.

Junior departments may operate just for Saturday morning or the whole day. A typical schedule might include tuition on both first and second study instrument, chamber music coaching, a theory and musicianship lesson, orchestral work and choral singing. Leading teachers and performers provide the expertise. Each element in the timetable adds a building block in musical awareness, says Heather Slade-Lipkin. 'Chamber music, for example, develops listening skills and reaction times under pressure. Singing develops musicality – it's vital to be able to pitch and sight-sing. Vocalising helps you so much in being able to phrase. We also take training for practice very seriously. We give advice on things like lighting, seating and how to break down practice time.'

Each junior department organises concerts as goals to work towards, inside and outside the conservatoire. There may also be whole weekend events, concentrating on a specialist area such as chamber music. Jonathan Willcocks nonetheless encourages pupils to keep up links with music-making in their own home areas. 'It's not for us to cherry-pick. Our pupils should take what they learn back into their youth orchestras and their school situations. That spreads the benefit and keeps them in contact with the "normal" world.'

Andrew Green and Kate Jones

See back of book for contact details

7. Choirs and choir schools

Who needs an instrument?

7

S O YOU RECKON singing is a second-best, soft option for your child? Hang on a moment! For a start, Chapter 3 showed that learning basic musical awareness through singing can be the surest way of rooting it in the subconscious and the gateway to so much else. Choristers at our leading cathedrals have plenty more about them than sweet voices; they are admired far and wide in refined circles for their virtuosity and musicality, maturity and self-confidence.

Then take a youth choir like the New London Children's Choir, which has tackled, without blinking, a whole string of pieces commissioned from leading contemporary composers. 'These composers weren't asked to write easier music just because it was a children's choir – the kids simply respond,' says conductor Ronald Corp. 'They come from all kinds of backgrounds; our training choir takes them without audition from the age of eight. Parents often bring children along saying they seem to sing a lot round the house. Very often they have no musical instrument on the go, possibly because of the situation in schools these days. They just soak up the training we can offer.'

He believes singing as part of children's education has been neglected in recent years. The Voices Foundation was set up as a charity to address the lack of singing expertise among teachers in primary schools. It now boasts an ever-expanding network of teachers from all disciplines who have received their special training: if you find your local school lacks any music specialist, you may wish to put them in touch (see back of book). 'The fact is that singing in a choir provides some of the best, and cheapest, musical training you can get,' says Ron Corp. 'The eye, ear, brain and vocal co-ordination that develops is high-

53

ly sophisticated, not to mention the skills of togetherness and precision. And children can make progress incredibly fast.'

The British Federation of Young Choirs will provide advice on what may be available in your local area. Its director, Susan Lansdale, says the situation nationwide is variable. 'A great deal depends on charismatic, inspired individuals. Singing has died a death in so many primary and middle schools and by the time children go on to secondary education they often find it socially and psychologically difficult to get involved in singing. Youth choirs stand for the idea that everyone can be trained to sing and a large number don't require auditions. It's very cheap to take part and these days the range of styles of music, representing so many different cultures and countries, is incredibly broad: anything goes. For so many kids, singing in a choir is a great confidence booster and it has a lively social side as well. Some choirs go on tour in the UK and abroad.'

Scoring goals in the choir stalls

The heyday of the parish church choir may be past, but the breed is far from dead with plenty enough activity to keep the Royal School of Church Music (RSCM) active in running holiday courses, chorister award schemes and goodness knows what else for girls as well as boys. From personal experience I have to say I'm amazed at how it's still possible in the Nineties for a young thug to be hacking a football around behind the vestry one moment and then actually allow himself to be transformed five minutes later into an angel wearing a ruff and flowing robes. 'When your friends in the choir look just like you it's not so bad,' suggests one of my chorister sons. His 13-year-old brother, now heavily into hair gel and designer trainers, reckons that the important thing was 'being introduced to the choir when I was seven. You don't think so much about it at that age and gradually you find you're involved. You make friends, play in the choir football team, and there are singing weeks and weekends away which are a bit like holidays.'

Many parish choirs offer excellent musical training with rich repertoire and graded awards. A lot also give concerts

Geoff Weaver, RSCM director of studies, says many parish choirs still offer an excellent musical training, with a wealth of repertoire from across the centuries to explore and graded awards to work for. 'The alertness and discipline called for are bound to benefit the children's general education. And there are different types of church choirs these days, not just the traditional ones, some of which only take boys. There are quite a few youth choirs attached to churches now and some of them travel around to sing services. Many parish choirs give concerts and deputise for cathedral choirs during the holidays. As you'd expect, a lot of the enjoyment will depend on the qualities of the individual choirmaster – it helps if they're in tune with the youngsters of today and make sure there's a range of social activities.'

Parents beware, though. Having a child singing in anything like a decent church choir will mess up your weekends and call for plenty of active support, including ferrying him or her to practices, weddings, choir-organised football matches and so on. But if a very young child seems to be getting a lot out of it, how about going full-time and becoming a chorister at one of Britain's cathedrals? Jane Capon of the Choir Schools' Association (CSA) reckons the cathedral choir

> Scholarships mean a child from any background can win a place as a cathedral chorister and have an excellent music education

schools she represents offer 'one of the best bargains in education. Not enough parents are aware of just what that can mean,' she says. 'Bursaries from the CSA or from individual cathedrals, or cash from the state choral scholarships scheme, mean that a child from any background can win a place as a cathedral chorister which carries with it a subsidised, excellent all-round education. That might then be followed by a music scholarship to a top independent school, which again may mean a subsidised general education right up to the age of 18. And there are increasingly more opportunities for girls at cathedrals such as Salisbury, Exeter and Wells. Choir school pupils invariably receive instrumental tuition as well. More choir schools now have a mixture of day-boys or girls and boarders and the catchment areas are much smaller. Many more schools now like parents of boarders to be in and out of the school supporting the child.'

Prospective choristers inevitably have to undergo an audition, but organists and choir school directors of music emphasise vehemently that they look for potential rather than a ready-trained, groomed product. 'We're after what you'd call "innate musicality",' says John Grundy, director of music at St Mary's Music School in Edinburgh, which provides the

---

ACTION POINTS

● Singing skills can be a very good basis for music learning generally

● Youth choirs tend to be committed to teaching all entrants to sing

● Many parish choirs give concerts and deputise at cathedrals, offering good performing experience

● If your child is a gifted singer a choir school can offer excellent subsidised education

● Membership of a choir is a time-consuming commitment, which increases greatly at choir school

boy and girl choristers for St Mary's Cathedral. 'The talent can be found in all kinds of family backgrounds. We do everything possible to make the audition unthreatening – in fact we make it fun with silly games, crazy singing activities; one exercise is just to read a book out loud. We hear what we need to hear.'

Most schools will also require a child to take an academic test. 'A child may have a golden voice,' warns Stephen Sides, headmaster of St Paul's Cathedral Choir School, 'but if there's continual tension over keeping up with school work alongside the demands of singing, there can be real trouble. It can be especially important that a chorister from a less privileged background can hack it academically. If they aren't able to win a scholarship to an independent school it can mean problems of adjustment back in the home and local school environment after they've maybe been a star at a cathedral.'

Singing in a cathedral or chapel is, Sides points out, a huge commitment. 'When parents write for a prospectus I deliberately try to put them off,' he says. 'There may be many benefits in terms of the education, the development of self-confidence and so on, but the down-side is that for five years the choristers are committed first and foremost to the Dean and Chapter of the cathedral, having short holidays, working at Christmas and Easter and working through long days. There are eight services a week plus concerts and recordings as well as two hours singing practice and lessons on two instruments a day. And parents get back a very different child from the one they delivered to us!'

If that sends a shiver down your spine, a number of cathedrals such as Bristol, Norwich and Wakefield have excellent voluntary choirs drawing on local day schools. It's still a marvellous musical education, involving services perhaps two or three days a week, even if you do have to wear a ruff and comb your hair now and again. *AG*

See back of book for contact details

8. Specialist schools

Havens or hothouses?

YOUR CHILD is racing ahead musically and enjoying it. Praise be! But possibly you feel the tuition that's within reasonable reach of home is not of the standard to stretch him or her as you'd like Perhaps the local school isn't sympathetic to your child's needs, including disruptions to studies caused by musical commitments. Musically gifted children can attract bullies, or it can simply be that they feel isolated in the school if they have no similarly musical friends. For these and other reasons, a specialist music school could be the answer.

There are five such schools which receive substantial funding from the government's music and ballet scheme: Chetham's School of Music in Manchester, the Purcell School at Bushey in Hertfordshire, St Mary's Music School in Edinburgh, the Yehudi Menuhin School at Stoke d'Abernon in Surrey and Wells Cathedral School Music School. All are affiliated to the new National Association of Music and Ballet Schools. Between them they offer some 550 pupil places. There is alsoone state school with a 'special music' unit attached – Pimlico School in London. Very few countries in the world have similar schools which place a specialist musical education within the context of a normal school curriculum.

All the specialist schools offer pupils tuition (on at least two instruments) and theory lessons, plus a range of other musical experiences, including orchestras and chamber music. The remainder of the curriculum may not be as broad as in most conventional schools, but will still be designed to more than meet the requirements of children seeking university entrance. Pupils arrive as early as age eight, the latest age for entry normally being 16 for the sixth-form years.

Nicolas Chisholm, headmaster of the Yehudi Menuhin School,

believes that too many parents with musical children have still to grasp the opportunity which the specialist schools can offer. 'We're especially looking for children with real musical potential from schools in the maintained sector – that's 90 per cent of the schools in this country. The cash from the government's music and ballet grant scheme has made all the difference and all pupils are eligible to benefit to some degree. Lack of money is no bar for parents. They pay a contribution to fees which is related to their salary. We have pupils whose parents are on income support and have nothing to pay at all.' Without grant assistance, average fees for the specialist schools come to around £16,000 per annum.

Securing a place

All the schools run auditions throughout the year. Candidates may have passed graded exams, but this is not a requirement. 'Have a go!' is Nicolas Chisholm's message to parents. 'Even if we can't offer a place we can always offer advice. I fear that many parents stand off a little thinking we must be rather snooty places, but all the schools work hard at being approachable. The auditions themselves will inevitably be fairly formal – the children will be coming on to a performance course so they simply have to play in front of a panel of adjudicators and must take certain aural tests. It's a competitive world. But we do all we can to take the pressure off. We interview child and parent together and if the parent is really keen but the child isn't motivated, I may well turn the candidate down.'

Music tuition at the specialist schools comes from a mixture of full-time and visiting staff, the latter likely to be players active in leading orchestras or chamber ensembles who may also teach at conservatoires.

According to John Baxter, headmaster of Wells Cathedral School and also chairman of the National Association of Music and Ballet Schools. 'As much care goes into selecting the staff teaching the rest of the curriculum. They have to be especially sensitive to the priority placed on music.'

If the parent is keen but the child is not motivated many schools will turn down the application to minimise pressure

For those wanting a more 'normal' school experience, Wells Cathedral School carries 170 specialist music students alongside 630 other pupils, all of whom (from as early as age three) benefit from the musical ethos, including the tuition available. Some even transfer to specialist status during their time at the school. The Wells curriculum is particularly broad and applicants must take an academic test. 'But we treat each case individually,' says John Baxter. 'A given pupil may not be as academically sharp as we'd like, but if he or she is an exceptional musician we can generally work around that.'

In London, the Pimlico School is a comprehensive offering a special musical curriculum. Westminster Council funds up to 15 specialist musical pupils per year and these fit their musical studies around the normal school curriculum.

However, while specialist schools may represent standards of excellence, that doesn't mean they will be appropriate for every gifted child. Some ex-pupils have questioned the wisdom of restricting the academic curriculum to devote at least a third of the day to music. Moreover, not everyone will be temperamentally suited to going away from home at an early age and facing the demanding routine expected at the schools. Nigel Kennedy has written movingly of his problems adjusting, at the age of seven, to life at the Yehudi Menuhin School in its early years. 'I met an utterly alien boarding school environment and lost forever what had previously been defined as home,' he recalls in his autobiography *Always Playing*. 'The school term seems to stretch on forever.' In his case, he claims, the rigorous routine cramped his natural style and he only made progress when practising alone in the evenings.

> The system could come as a shock to younger children: you have to train for five hours a day

Bobby Chen, an 18-year-old pianist currently studying at the school agrees that the system is tough going and could come as a shock to younger children. 'You have to train for at least five hours a day, starting at 8am, and fit the academic timetable in as well,' he says. 'I did have more difficulty doing my A-levels than I otherwise would have had, but while you are encouraged to work very hard there is great support; the teachers are like parents.'

Flautist Juliette Bausor, a finalist at this year's BBC Young Musicians competition, went to the Purcell School at the age of 14 and, although she enjoyed the experience, she warns parents to be cautious: 'Fourteen was the right age for me because I'm very home-loving and if I'd gone before I wouldn't have enjoyed it at all,' she says. 'Pushing children into something like this against their will, I'm sure, causes problems. They are likely to rebel in some way and academic work can suffer. My feeling is that if you haven't set your mind on making music a major part of your life, or maybe your career, then you should think twice about going to a specialist school.'

Life as a boarder

Being few in number, the specialist schools inevitably carry significant numbers of boarders. Nicolas Chisholm understands that prospective parents may be concerned about a child starting boarding as early as eight, but still believes that the earlier a child can begin the better. 'You have to remember that many of them have been in school environments which are in effect "abnormal" to them, where music has no special place,' he says. 'Here they enter a "normal" situation. If you're especially talented at a young age it's all the more important to make absolutely sure that bad habits don't creep into the playing. So many orchestra musicians these days report physical problems which often relate to poor posture or technique which weren't tackled when they were young. Musical considerations apart, this isn't a threatening atmosphere even for a very young student. There are only 54 places at the school, so there's a family atmosphere. And we make it a policy that all boarders should get out of the school once a week to visit parents or a guardian.'

A typical day at Wells Cathedral School starts with pupils tackling an hour and a half of individual practice from 7.45am. The school day proper, consisting of eight timetabled lessons, then begins. Within that day the music students fit in three hours of specialist study, including such elements as theory, chamber music and individual tuition (there are two hours per week of one-to-one teaching on a first instrument) achieved by selective opting out of particular lessons such as sport or religious education. There will be plenty of musical activity in the evenings to fit in around prep, including playing at events both inside and away from the school, or visits to professional concerts. Singing is taken very seriously as a vital adjunct to instrumental training. All the specialist schools pride themselves on taking a range of homegrown ensembles, orchestras or choirs on tour both in the UK and abroad.

John Baxter is anxious to stave off any suggestion that children in specialist music schools live an isolated, ivory-tower existence. 'For example, it's vital we forge links with the local area. As organisations receiving amounts of government cash we have the responsibility to put something back into music. It's an attitude shared by all the specialist schools. Here at Wells we have links to a community school in a tough area of Bristol. We're working on joint projects together, which have involved

---

ACTION POINTS

● There are five specialist music schools which receive funding from the government's music and ballet scheme

● Lack of money is no bar. Parents' contribution fees are related to their salary

● Most look for musical potential rather than precocious technique

● Music training takes up about a third of the day, which can mean the academic curriculum is less broad

● Schools have sometimes been condemned as hothouses. Hours of work are very long, but there is usually a family atmosphere

their tremendous steel band.'

Scotland is served not only by the government-assisted St Mary's Music School in Edinburgh, but by two specialist schools funded by their local authorities (thereby charging no fees): the City of Edinburgh Music School and the Music School of Douglas Academy in Glasgow. Both are members of the National Association of Music and Ballet Schools. The Edinburgh Music School prides itself on catering for all styles of music, including bagpipes, rock guitar and drums. Specialist tuition for the 50 or so pupils is based in well-equipped music units attached to two existing Edinburgh day schools (one primary, one secondary) with strong musical traditions of their own – Flora Stevenson Primary and Broughton High respectively. Music tuition largely comes from visiting and part-time staff, many of whom also visit other specialist schools or junior departments at conservatoires. 'Because of our links with the Flora Stevenson and Broughton High schools we can offer pupils a wide curriculum,' says director of music Tudor Morris, 'and the music students get the benefit of spending much of their day with pupils of very different backgrounds.' *AG*

8

See back of book for contact details

9. Music scholarships to independent schools

When the piper pays the fees

IF YOU HAVE a child of around ten whose musical talents are already obvious, you will be looking for a school which will encourage and nurture them. The advantage of sending your child to the local state secondary is that the school day is often shorter and your child will get more practice time at home. He or she may also benefit from the numerous outreach programmes run by professional orchestras and opera companies, including composing projects and workshops run by musicians, who get financial backing for community and education programmes.

On the other hand, your child might do well at an independent school with a thriving music department and a reputation for musical achievement. If you're worried about how you will afford the fees, a music scholarship might be the way forward. The opportunities offered by the better independent schools are often too good to refuse. Many professional musicians would give their eye-teeth for the state-of-the-art practice rooms, rehearsal studios and concert halls some schools enjoy. They see it as part of their job to attract musical pupils and their atmosphere can be encouraging, energetic and musically inspirational. Of course, not all independent schools have amazing facilities or an inspiring musical ethos, but those that give substantial music scholarships may be hoping to boost their reputation for music and 'generate enthusiasm and raise the performing levels' as one director of music puts it. They offer a substantial reduction in fees in the hope of tempting the musical stars of the future.

A good school will give your child a chance to blossom in the company of other musicians, to get excellent tuition (Uppingham was recently compared with a specialist music school for its conservatoire-level teaching) and plenty of opportunity to play in orchestras, take part in musical productions and sing in choirs. As one head of music put it, 'singing is in the woodwork'. Music scholars may progress to the National Youth Orchestra, or win a university place as a choral scholar. Or perhaps they won't take music any further, but will have the option to continue it for pleasure throughout their life.

Requirements for scholarship

Most candidates for musical scholarship will be outstanding on one instrument and will show promise on a second. Auditions are mostly competitive, so a child who plays only one instrument may not be taken seriously by some schools. Directors of music may ask for Grade 6 at the age of 12, others look for potential, enthusiasm and no grades at all. Most do specify some sort of grade because it gives people a rough guide to the standard required. But as one head of music points out, this has its drawbacks. 'The difference between Grade 4 with distinction and Grade 6 pass is enormous. I'd rather have the former. There's also a danger that if you insist on Grade 5 or 6, the school puts pressure on the pupil to push them through the grades. That isn't what we want.' Christopher Francis, director of music at Badminton Girls' School, agrees. 'We're looking for the foundations of technique, not terrifically advanced players.'

Until recently details of music scholarships around the country were hard to get hold of, but now there's an invaluable guide called *Music Awards at Independent Senior Schools* (see back of book for details). It has page-long entries on 143 schools, with details of the music department, number and size of scholarships on offer, standard required and a thumbnail sketch of the facilities and musical achievements of each school. It lists in less detail over 130 other schools offering scholarships.

Many schools are looking for the foundations of technique, not only very advanced young players

Do you choose a school for its excellent reputation for music, or because you want your child to go to it anyway, even though it's not particularly well known for music? I was keen for my son to go to a London day school, which meant rejecting some of the best schools for music in the country. If, however, your child is happy to board and you are happy to let them, the choice is far wider and the entry requirements are often more flexible. Many heads of music would say that musical and academic ability go hand in hand, but it's worth checking that your child is likely to get through any academic entry requirements before setting your heart on a fiercely academic school. Most London schools, and others like Winchester and Eton, have stiff entry exams (or Common Entrance requirements) which all scholarship candidates must pass, as well as auditioning.

Once you have narrowed down your search to the schools that might suit your child, the next step is to get in touch with the head of music. All, without exception, are anxious to meet parents and find out what their child might have to offer. Tony Henwood at Latymer Upper School in West London says, 'I don't want anyone to be put off. If they're interested, I urge them to come and see me. I want to hear as many children as possible.' Find out when it's appropriate to take your child along – some schools like to see them a year before they're due to audition, some prefer to leave it until the term before. If you are going to look round the school anyway, make a point of meeting the head of music and finding out more about musical life at school, the variety of orchestras, productions, etc. If possible, sound them out about demand for the instrument that your child plays. When I took my son, an oboist, round our chosen school, the head of music let drop that they were looking for a second oboe in the main orchestra and I immediately knew that Jack's chances were better than if he'd played the clarinet!

Some schools are prepared to accept a lower standard on rarer instruments such as the bassoon or the tuba

9

It's not just the standard of playing that counts when it comes to allotting awards. Directors of music have to be pragmatic about the instruments they need for their orchestra, and although some would deny that they favour some instruments over others, many make no bones about it. 'Orchestral players, particularly on rarer instruments like the viola, oboe, bassoon and horn, certainly have an advantage over the piano and the guitar,' says one director of music. Some schools are definitely prepared to take a lower standard on rarer instruments such as the bassoon or the tuba. 'Everyone has a problem finding strings, so if you play the violin or viola, you'll be in demand,' says another director.

Many schools give special consideration to cathedral choristers, particularly if they can still sing treble. Some schools are prepared to count the voice as a second instrument, others expect instrumentalists to be able to sing anyway. Nigel Horsfall at Sedbergh would never rule out a boy who offered voice as an instrument. 'If you get a singer with a good ear, who has real musicality, you know that you can teach him an orchestral instrument.' Other heads of music see it differently; they take for granted that instrumental players will be musical all-rounders, so make no special effort to attract choral singers. The choir of Trinity School in Croydon is known for its work with English National Opera and other high profile productions, so it attracts singers. Head of mus: David Squibb says, 'There's an emphasis on instrumental scholarship because boys want to come here anyway for the choir. They can g(choral awards once they've got here if they prove themselves.'

Singing for their supper

If the school gives your child a music scholarship, what is he or sh expected to give the school in return? Will it involve hours of extra wor and appearance in every concert? Is it, in short, a form of slavery? Not ; all, claim most heads of music. The idea is that they should 'participat fully in the musical life of the school,' which usuall

The scholarship may be a reward for doing well, but in fact the child must work very hard to justify it

means a choir, an orchestra and whatever smalle ensembles are appropriate. 'There's no documer saying scholars will do GCSE music,' says one. 'The usually want to take part anyway,' says anothe Jasper Thorogood, head of music at Felsted, is mad of sterner stuff. 'When I first came to the school, th feeling was that the children had done very well an(

the scholarship was a sort of reward. I made it quite clear I expected them to sing for their supper! They have to work very hard – to take th(lead and set the standard for everyone who plays.'

Most directors of music agree that a music scholar has to be good a time management to fit in academic work, instrumental lessons (usually during academic lessons, taken on a rota basis), music practice, playing in orchestras/ensembles/choirs and doing homework, with sport and hobbies on top. Nigel Horsfall at Sedbergh says being a music scholar is quite a commitment, 'but if I was a parent, I'd want my child to be under some sort of pressure. The rewards are that when they're in a performance that's gone particularly well they feel they're taking part in something a bit special.'

There are slightly fewer opportunities for girls to win scholarships: of the 143 schools listed in detail in the guide to music awards, 37 are all-girls schools, 43 are all-boys (some with

ACTION POINTS

● Many independent schools have music facilities professionals would covet

● A scholarship candidate who plays only one instrument might not be taken seriously by some schools

● If your child is prepared to board the choice is wider and entry requirements often more flexible

● Always meet the head of music at your chosen school and ask about the variety of orchestras and productions

● Remember a scholarship pupil must fit in music lessons, practice and rehearsals around their academic work

girls in the sixth form) and the remainder are co-ed. But the richest schools do tend to be long-established boys' schools such as Eton. Many parents would admit to having sent their sons to choir schools because it will increase their chance of a music scholarship as well as giving them an excellent musical grounding. It is only recently that girls have been allowed into choir schools. Directors of music are looking with interest at the latest batch of girl choristers coming out of Salisbury Cathedral School, for example, many of whom have gained music awards at independent schools. 'Girls work harder and are more diligent and I think they'll be getting the scholarships in the future,' says the head of music at a choir school which has recently started to take girls. 'Whether or not girls get scholarships, more of them take music seriously. The percentage of pupils taking weekly music lessons at girls' schools is much higher than at boys'.'

The price of an independent school education can be alleviated, or even removed altogether, by a music scholarship. But the costs remain high. Boarding fees in 1997/8 ranged from around £8,000 to £14,000 a year; day fees were anything from £5,000 to £10,000 a year. Music awards vary from a £50 exhibition to free music tuition (worth about £100 a term for one instrument), to 50 per cent of boarding fees, topped up in some cases to full fees (all scholarships at Eton can be supplemented to full fees). Christ's Hospital School, in West Sussex, makes a point of offering bursaries to parents who would not be able to afford the £11,000 a year fees – between 30 and 40 per cent of parents pay nothing at all. Music is a high priority at the school and free instrumental tuition is available to many pupils. Details of the number and size of awards at other schools appear in the aforementioned *Music Awards at Independent Senior Schools. Amanda Holloway*

See back of book for contact details

10. Summer courses

A guide to harmonious holidays

IF THE PROSPECT OF weekly orchestra rehearsals or Saturdays at a conservatoire junior department (see Chapter 6) doesn't render your offspring catatonic, what about something to keep the blood racing out of term-time? The growth of an independent sector running residential and non-residential courses and camps in the school holidays, especially the summer, has been a feature of the last 30 years or so. The *Music Education Yearbook* (see back of book for details) lists dozens of such events, of which a healthy proportion cater for the younger age group. Practically everything is dealt with in musical terms, from orchestral and ensemble playing to specialist courses for particular instruments, from singing courses and early music to jazz (see Chapter 11). It's very likely there will be something somewhere that's appropriate to both your child's interest and ability level. Fees inevitably vary, but organisers bend over backwards to offer assistance in cases of financial hardship.

Why add to the slog of practice, school choir and youth orchestra by signing up for yet more in the summer hols? Here are some thoughts on the benefits from a variety of course directors. Early on the scene, in 1969, was the Pro Corda Trust. Its mission remains that of improving playing in orchestras by offering talented young string players specialist tuition in chamber music, essentially string quartets. Selected by audition from across the UK, players attend summer courses at Leiston in Suffolk, ideally from the age of eight. Youngsters return year by year as they work their way through a range of ability levels up to the age of 18. 'Many young players just jog along in their youth orchestras,' says co-founder Pamela Spofforth. 'At Leiston they get away with nothing. It's one person per part, you have to do all your own counting and yc can't get away with poor intonation and sound production.'

Some of the locations of summer schools are s

beguiling – say Bude, Guernsey or the Lake District that it might pay parents to take a cottage nearby ar make a family affair out of it all, not least when comes to trooping along to the concert(s) th inevitably round off the week. The Marlboroug College Summer School holds weekly cours throughout the summer for beginners, intermediate and more advanced students, plus over 140 cours

which can include the family. HF Holidays Ltd is a private compar offering a wide variety of music-making and music-appreciatio holidays throughout the year, including 'Singing for the Tone Deaf', s lack of musical confidence needn't be a handicap.

There is a range of schools dedicated to one instrument including th Andover Harp Course, the Double Bass Summer School, the Gatherir of the Clans, which organises cello courses and masterclasses at venue around the country, the Oxford Cello School, the Oundle Internation Festival and the Summer School for Young Organists. Founder/directe of the Oxford Cello School, Marianne Gottfeldt, runs a series of resider tial courses in July and August for different ability levels from advance down to beginners. She says there are immense benefits to be gaine from a period of intensive study alongside people who also pla your instrument. Especially there's the stimulation of seeing how you playing differs from somebody else's. 'Every student has been taught b a different teacher, each of whom inevitably offers different insights she says. 'As ideas are shared you're forced to think for yourself and tr new things.'

The downside is that single-instrument schools may not offer chance to play in a group with different instruments or to learn othe skills – and the rewards of playing in an ensemble entirely made up c flutes can be somewhat limited. The benefits of the more general kin of summer school is that within a tightly-knit environment there will b a huge range of musicians of all ages and abilities. They may be polishing their talents through masterclasses and workshops on variou instruments, or learning all sorts of skills from practical conducting piano accompaniment and jazz improvisation to Alexander Techniqu and T'ai Chi. Often, if your child has his or her own chamber musi group, they can all go to these courses together.

Summer courses are held all over the country, from the Llandaf Summer Music Course in Wales to the Beauchamp House Holiday Musi

Summer courses

Courses in Gloucester and courses run by the Scottish Amateur Music Association.

The National Children's Music Camps take place each summer in the grounds of the Old Rectory, Wavendon in Buckinghamshire, home territory for Cleo Laine and John Dankworth, whose sister Avril is the NCMC's founder/director. There are four camps each summer, two for juniors (8-12) and two for teenagers (13-17), each consisting of 32 boys and 32 girls. The music experienced covers folk, jazz, classical, pop, electronic, vocal and instrumental. 'Collaboration is the name of the game, not individual tuition,' says administrator David Edwards. 'The huge benefit is what they learn about co-operation and socialising. The children are graded by ability and work together in ensembles, orchestras, or maybe on an operetta, or on improvisation. Tutors are able to rewrite things for any ability. Parents say that children grow up dramatically in a week and they come back year after year.'

> Collaboration is the focus at summer school. Often it provides children with a first chance to play in an orchestra

Sing for Pleasure runs residential weekends and summer schools in venues around the country for children of all abilities from age ten to 18. There are no auditions. The younger ages will be introduced to group singing through drama and music games, building up to a concert. The organisation is particularly keen to link to the school situation. 'We're well aware,' says director Alan Jefferis, 'of how tricky things are in schools where the music "specialist" may have little musical background at all. Very often a group of children will come with a teacher.'

Teachers have become increasingly entrepreneurial in recent years and no organisation proves the point more obviously than David and Gillian Johnston's Musicale Holidays. Musicale runs 20 five-day non-residential courses around the country. Children can start as young as age five. Each course is split into two sections. Children on the 'music activity course' have yet to play an

10

ACTION POINTS

● Summer schools combine musical learning experience with many social, cultural and sports events

● For some children they offer the first opportunity to play in an orchestra

● Single-instrument courses focus the mind and allow students to compare technique, but they don't offer the benefits of playing in a mixed ensemble

● Courses range from three days to three weeks. Most schools are residential and can be expensive

● If your child does not feel up to the social whirl they may benefit from a short non-residential course or workshop

● The intensity of such courses can give children a vital stimulus

instrument – they take part in a range of activities, including writing and drawing as well as playing simple musical instruments and singing. The instrumental course caters for complete beginners up to around Grade 5 level, providing the opportunity to play in ensembles of various kinds. 'For many children it proves a good way of starting an interest in music,' says David Johnston. 'They associate music with a great experience - the whole social side, the games, the swimming pool and so on. I reckon some of the children pack a year's practice into a week and some are thrilled by their first chance of playing in an orchestra. Parents write and say that their child has turned a corner in their attitude to music when they go home; they can't put their instrument down!'

Courses vary in duration from three days to three weeks, and in entry requirements depending on the course. The majority are residential and therefore can be expensive, particularly if specific music needs to be bought and prepared in advance.

If your child does not feel up to the social whirl of a summer music course or suffers from chronic homesickness, they might benefit from a short non-residential course or workshop. Many of the institutions which hold longer vacation courses, such as the Lake District Summer School, the Midland Arts Centre and Stringwise in London, also offer day workshops for young students. There are also one-day workshops for specialist interests such as Sing for Pleasure, based in Essex. More general short courses include Musicale Holidays (held all over the country), the Islington Arts Factory and the Lancaster Rehearsal Orchestra.

The range is immense, but any well-run course can provide a musically, culturally and personally enriching experience that will not be forgotten, whether or not it leads to a musical career. And it certainly beats Play Station! *KJ/AG*

See back of book for contact details

11. Jazz and rock

Striking a more informal note

NOT SO LONG AGO youth culture was inclined to dismiss jazz as the domain of nerds in lumpy jumpers and ageing swingers revisiting their youth, while conservatives refused to recognise it as a serious art form. In the last ten years, however, jazz has been swiftly regaining its street cred. Universities have begun offering degree courses dedicated to it, schools are clearing space in the curriculum for jazz workshops and graded exams for jazz instruments and ensembles have just been launched by the Associated Board of the Royal Schools of Music. 'We are having more and more requests for jazz workshops because kids are getting to hear the music through artists like Julian Joseph, who are recording pop records,' says Adrian Tilbrook of Jazz Action, a group funded by Northern Arts and Yorkshire and Humberside Arts to promote jazz in the region.

Pop may not have had the same stigma among the young, but even so it is only now gaining ground in school timetables. Formal training is anathema to purists, but if your eight-year-old is set on playing the electric guitar it helps to point him or her in the right direction.

The official recognition of both genres is good news for parents who have to frogmarch their offspring on to the piano stool, for the liberated nature of the music can often seduce reluctant musicians. Rather than spending a month being drilled in scales and notation, children are usually encouraged to improvise in their first lesson. 'The only thing you can lay down the law about is timing,' says Ian Carr, eminent trumpeter and jazz writer who directs weekly jazz workshops on the Weekend Arts Course at the Interchange in London. 'Jazz is all about the person who is playing it and their imagination.'

Ginny Macbeth, who runs a music publicity agency in London, had decided against paying for music lessons for her children before she happened upon a local jazz workshop. Now she has enrolled her eight-year-old daughter in jazz piano lessons at school. 'Kids are really pushed academically at school and I didn't want to add yet another subject to the timetable,' she says. 'But jazz is much more informal, like playing tennis after school, and it's fun, while classical music lessons often are not. It's also a good basis for learning classical music because children can feel at home with an instrument more quickly.'

Jazzing up tuition

Unfortunately, the quality and availability of jazz tuition across the country is still patchy and, although it is included in the GCSE syllabus, where improvisation is now encouraged, whether or not it is provided by individual schools depends on the personal taste and ability of the music teacher. Because universities have only recently begun to launch formal jazz courses, many school teachers have no experience of it themselves and are ill-equipped to teach a new generation. Jazz Services, funded by the Arts Council of England, is campaigning to improve the situation and has applied for lottery money to supply every school with a book and a CD-ROM advising on teaching facilities. There are also regional jazz services which organise workshops and keep a database of teachers and courses.

However, one of the reasons why jazz has had to wait so long for recognition as a valid academic subject is because of dissent within the jazz world itself. A hard core of musicians insist that jazz, by its very nature, cannot be taught and that those who try will end up homogenising its sound. Almost all of the great names such as Louis Armstrong and Miles Davis picked up their technique by trial and error and consequently developed their own unique sound. But educators like Richard Michael, who teaches improvisation at the Royal Scottish Academy of Music and Drama, dismiss such objections as unfounded. 'My ideal musician has the technique of a classical musician with the ears of a jazz musician. We want to get people away from the fear of hearing Oscar Peterson or Keith Jarrett and thinking "how can I play this?" The answer is, start with simple scales and sequences and progress from there.'

The London College of Music now offers graded exams in jazz saxophone and the Guildhall School of Music has syllabuses for saxophone and jazz clarinet. The Associated Board, which sent out a nationwide survey

Regional jazz services organise workshops in schools and keep a database of teachers and courses

before deciding to initiate its jazz piano syllabus, received 6,000 enquiries within a month of the launch. Improvisation is a key element of each grade and students are supplied with a CD of backing music so they can practise rhythm and harmonies at home. Moreover, there is provision for children who can't read music to play pieces by ear. 'There is great excitement that you can know almost nothing about music and can just start playing jazz,' says British jazz pianist Julian Joseph. 'This new syllabus will give everyone a chance to understand what's going on and not to think that we all just woke up one morning and started to play.'

Jazz may give the impression of laid-back ease, but it requires as much dedication and technical skill as classical music

Be warned, however, for jazz may give the impression of laid-back ease, but it requires just as much dedication and technical skill as classical music. The important thing is to distinguish between a wish to learn and a wish to play. Your child might want to blast on a trumpet like Dizzy Gillespie but would baulk at the years of practice required. Once you've established that the ambition is genuine you should approach the music teacher at your child's school. If he or she cannot advise you, your local music service might, or else you can contact Jazz Services, which keeps a database on peripatetic teachers and courses in your area. It is a good idea to start with a workshop where the child can get a feel for different instruments and types of music. As musical styles converge and jazz composers write increasingly for classical ensembles, the range of instruments is ever broadening – even bagpipes can apply! However, it's worth starting with one, such as drums, clarinet, piano, guitar, bass guitar, percussion or trumpet, which is common to most areas of repertoire.

11

The world of jazz music is a bewildering labyrinth for the uninitiated. The term incorporates 'Dixieland' (the Chicago-style jazz of the Twenties), bebop, hard bop, mainstream (as in the music of Duke Ellington), fusion and jazz rock (played on amplified instruments), Latin jazz, drum and bass (a new trend) and several dozen more variations. If your child wants to focus on a specific, less mainstream style, Jazz Services should be able to help find a teacher who specialises in it.

For a more intensive introduction, there are a number of excellent summer schools offering one- to two-week courses. The Guildhall Summer School provides a week's grounding in jazz, rock and studio music for beginners aged 12 and above; Michael Garrick, professor of jazz piano at the Royal Academy runs the Jazz Academy Vacation Course in Tunbridge Wells where enthusiasts of all ages and ability can involve themselves in play-along sessions, teachers of various instruments are on hand for tuition and there are evening concerts by Garrick and others. The Jazz College in Clitheroe, Lancashire, operates along similar lines and, in Aberdeen, the Grampian Jazz School runs courses for all ages throughout the year. For students over 16, Paul McCartney's Liverpool Institute of Performing Arts runs an international summer school with separate one- and two-week courses on jazz, rock song-writing and studio rock with the opportunity to spend five days in a recording studio. Most courses culminate in a live performance by the students.

Whatever form of tuition you choose, your child is likely to come away from his or her first lesson having produced a piece of music, even if they have never touched an instrument before. 'My first lessons always encourage improvisation,' says Richard Crozier, a teacher and director of professional development at the Associated Board. 'You can make a good effect with a very few notes. Music education tends to focus very heavily on notation, but overlooks the element of play which children love.' He recommends beginners start off in a workshop where they can pick up tips from their peers. 'You can go straight into chords with a group and the kids can provide backing while the teacher improvises.'

Rocking the boat

Rock music has also begun gaining ground in schools, though independent schools are often more traditional in their approach. In Coventry, the Performing Arts Service has dispatched a professional rock band into over half the local state schools to provide ongoing tuition and several of the schools have since set up their own pop groups. Several of the professional boy bands do occasional rounds in schools across the country, but these sessions tend to be one-offs and geared more to promoting the latest record, although they might serve to galvanise their youthful audience. Some performers such as Herbie Flowers, who runs occasional clinics in schools in Sussex, receive local authority funding to educate the next generation. However, rock tuition is as controversial as jazz among those who are worried that popular culture will become 'academicised'. 'There is an argument that as soon as pop is taught in schools it ceases to be pop,' says soloist and teacher Charlie Beale. 'You have to allow a student to control his own learning and improvise, and this is something classical music education could learn from.' Certainly, formal qualifications are by no means a necessity, especially if the student already has a thorough grounding in a classical instrument. Ben Ross, who learnt the violin as a child and now has his own band, taught himself the bass guitar by playing along to Police records. 'I wanted to get away from doing grades and be cool playing with the lads,' he says. 'Unless you want to go professional you don't even need to learn notation if you play rock.'

Simon Pitt, who runs Rock School, a specialist examining board in

Richmond, Surrey, is adamant that formal teaching is the way forward. 'In the old days you made it up as you went along but that won't work any more,' he says. 'Bands in schools that do the graded exams tend to progress faster. It sets them attainment targets and teaches them the huge range of possibilities which they would take years to work out for themselves.'

Over 300 colleges now offer BTEC courses in popular music and performance but as yet only two institutions offer graded exams in the field. The Registry of Guitar Teachers has bass and guitar exams validated by the London College of Music, and six years ago the Rock School established exams in electric guitar, bass and drums, validated by Trinity College of Music. Both keep a database of rock teachers nationwide and are a good first port of call if your school is more Beethoven-oriented. Unlike jazz, there are no funded educational services dedicated to rock and the supply of good teachers is patchy. 'I reckon it will take ten years for the idea of rock exams to get established and another ten to produce enough qualified teachers to get things moving,' says Simon Pitt.

As with jazz, though, workshops are perhaps the best way to get the feel of band life and to experiment with different instruments. The Power House in Acton now lodges the Guitar Institute and four specialist schools, Basstech, Drumtech, Vocaltech and Keyboardtech, all of which provide full-time courses for school-leavers and tuition, assessments and events for younger students. Further north, the Birmingham Institute of Guitar runs a ten-week course for eight- to 15-year-olds consisting of an hour's tuition every Friday and its summer school is especially aimed at young beginners. The recently founded Academy of Contemporary Music in Guildford has set up a GCSE equivalent for the truly dedicated: attendance at a year-long Saturday school should yield a certificate in popular music validated by the Open College Network. Those preferring a more relaxed pace can enrol in a once-weekly evening class for all ages and abilities which runs for four ten-week terms and includes a band skills course. *Anna Tims*

See back of book for contact details

11

ACTION POINTS

● The liberated nature of jazz and rock lessons can often seduce reluctant young musicians

● Jazz Services offers a database of teachers and workshops nationwide

● Workshops are a good starting point as they enable children to play as a band and sample different instruments

● The new jazz and rock graded exams place emphasis on improvisation and experiment

● Many prefer to learn jazz and rock as a hobby without the pressure of lessons and exams

12. World music

Broadening the horizons

MOST MUSICIANS know the feeling. You hear some music, go to a performance, see the instrument that makes the magic sounds and think 'I have to play that'. But what do you do when you have fallen in love with a kora, or a pair of tablas, and you don't know anyone who can teach you? Not so long ago the answer was often to hand at school, particularly in cities. When the peripatetic teaching system was dismantled, Asian and African instruments were usually among the first to be dropped. There is now an enormous un-fulfilled appetite for experiencing them, as any world music performing group soon discovers if it offers education workshops.

However, there is plenty of music happening in Britain without any direct help from the education system. Communities always have ways of keeping things going, although outsiders won't always know about it unless it is advertised to them. Find out about musicians in the style you like who live in the area or who are visiting. Go and see them play, meet them afterwards and ask them what's around. Many world music groups often give workshops connected with performances, and some-body will eventually know somebody who gives lessons.

Serious study of a non-Western musical tradition can be enlightening in a number of ways. The method of teaching will probably be rather different from any that you might have already been used to, often concentrating more on practical skills rather than on any attempt to explain theory – that comes later. If you're thinking of learning an Indian instrument, for example, expect a kind of apprenticeship, and a close relationship with your teacher; Indonesian gamelan, on the other hand, is more of a social activity, stressing group interaction and an all-round ability to play the many instruments. Inevitably this kind of study also shows music in a different cultural context – in other cultures, music often serves a particular function, or may be strongly associated with other art forms – and this in itself can shed new light on the role of music within our own culture. And for budding composers, study of the way music is created round the world can open their eyes to all kinds of possibilities: new sounds, new techniques, new instruments. You never know, it might even encourage you to write a piece for sitar or mbira.

In places with concentrated populations, the focus of musical activity is often a community centre. London's Chinatown has specific music shops as well as cultural organisations. Among South Asians, the music instruction may be centred on a temple or gurdwara. Local good-quality players will give lessons there to beginners and occasionally a distinguished international performer will visit. If the activity is well organised it can link into examination systems quite similar to the graded exams in Western music. Leeds, for instance, has a network of connections that lead from local centres to the Leeds College of Music, which has foundation courses and full-time undergraduate-level students. A new academy of Indian music and dance is growing from this basis and will soon have a wider impact on the national scene. Elsewhere the Bharatiya Vidya Bhavan in west London, a well-known centre for Indian culture, hosts music lessons and classes and has as many Western students of all ages as Asians.

> **Formal courses after school age are limited. Colleges and universities have a better record than conservatoires**

Options for study

At present the formal options for studying world music after school age are limited. Of the conservatoires, only Birmingham is active in developing its provision, which is now part of every student's experience and has put down firm local roots. This is a substantial and wide-ranging operation which complements the more specific work at the Leeds college. The older conservatoires have not stirred themselves in this direction and Britain still lacks anything to match the world music department at Rotterdam Conservatoire. Here there are several specialist sub-departments and ensembles of professional standard which have made commercial recordings, particularly in Latin American music.

A few universities and colleges make a good showing. The more detached pursuit of ethnomusicology has long had a place in the syllabus, but many kinds of music are now studied in a direct or hands-on way. The School of Oriental and African Studies in London spans these approaches for the music of a range of cultures from the Middle

12

East to east Asia, with a well-known specialist staff (often heard in Radio 3's Sunday evening world music programme) and good contacts among UK-resident and visiting performers. York University is strong on several areas from Africa to the Pacific – senior lecturer Neil Sorrell is an authority on Indian and Indonesian musics – and has hosted residencies by leading musicians such as Amjad Ali Khan. Some of the more diverse courses in newer universities, such as City University, give at least a proportion of their time, while among the higher education colleges Dartington has had a long-established strand and King Alfred's College in Winchester actually specialises in practical courses that study several world traditions from performing, creative and theoretical perspectives.

An odd coincidence of cultural relations and gifts has seen to it that Indonesian gamelans crop up in an impressively large number of places. In the last few years, they have become an important part of music education because of the listening skills and group interaction that the music requires. Several schools and local music authorities own gamelans now, but if you want to take study further, think of York, Durham, Oxford or Cambridge universities, or Dartington. You can also find flourishing non-university groups in Edinburgh, Glasgow and Manchester. In London, the South Bank Centre is the focal point for a very active gamelan education programme – classes for all ages and all levels of ability happen seven days a week.

As in the West, serious performers in most forms of music undergo a training that lasts many years. In India the established tradition of learning amounts to a residential apprenticeship. Aspiring players may have to be prepared to spend time in the home milieu of their music, whatever their own cultural origin. Some countries even invite foreign students by offering them scholarships to study their traditional arts: try contacting the appropriate embassy. In the past people have got away with calling themselves experts after a few weeks in the company of an African master drummer, but nobody swallows that line any more. A short commitment can leave you well informed, but you will always remain on the outside.

One word of warning. Outside the UK, and among the more traditionally minded here, it is hard for players of wholly European origin without any family links to the cul-

> **ACTION POINTS**
>
> ● World music provision is patchy, but a good place to start is community centres
>
> ● Remember that methods of teaching are very different, ranging from apprenticeship to group learning
>
> ● Most major cities in Britain have a gamelan. The South Bank gamelan in London has a particularly active programme

ture to be accepted on equal terms with those born into it. You should expect as a player to live to a certain extent within your cultural limitations. That doesn't mean you will have an unrewarding time. As cultures mix more and more you will have great experiences in musical encounters with traditionally trained performers, whether on your ground or theirs. Many modern percussion groups have shown a way forward, and do much good educational work. And if it is the music that grabs you as much as the instrument there are more imaginative possibilities still, such as cross-cultural performance in which two forms interact, or learning to play a Western instrument in another world style. The saxophone and violin work particularly well in Indian music, as players from both the West and India have been discovering. Trust your creative spirit, and who knows where you will go?

Robert Maycock

See back of book for contact details

12

13. The budding composer

Learning about music through writing it yourself

NOT SO LONG AGO composition was something practised only by an initiated few, and then strictly in the privacy of their own homes. It was rather a mysterious business. It could not be found on any school syllabus and if you asked about it, you'd probably be told that the world already had all the composers it needed and that virtually all of them were dead. Then, with the advent of the GCSE in 1988, composition was wrested out of its obscure corner and placed firmly at the heart of the curriculum where it continues to make up a third of the current GCSE syllabus. It's a change which reflects, as teacher and composer Philip Flood puts it, the idea of 'teaching through making. You can't understand how music works unless you do it yourself.'

The change from the older pedagogy, with its emphasis on written work and abstruse theory, to the present-day love of making and doing is not unique to music – it's rather like the way language teaching has shifted from the grammatical to the practical – but it also reflects some of the wider arguments about what sort of music is actually worth teaching. One of the problems, according to composer and workshop leader Colin Riley, is that we have 'so many kinds of music nowadays that we don't have an educational structure to deal with them'. Pop, jazz, world music, and new technology are all elbowing their way into the curriculum and into pupils' compositions, inevitably at the expense of traditional studies. The problem is not only how to teach, but what.

One indicator or the change is the new importance of music technology in composition. Virtually every school nowadays has some kind of music workstation – usually consisting of a keyboard hitched to a computer running one or more sampling, sequencing or music-setting programmes (CUBASE, Logic or, most recently, Sibelius are typical). Using the keyboard, pupils can play their music directly into the computer and then manipulate it electronically – cutting, splicing, sequencing, layering. Packages also come with libraries of digitalised instrumental and rhythmic 'samples', so that students can access the sounds of anything from a set of bagpipes to a euphonium. The computer will even notate pieces automatically and print out a score, so there's no need even to know how music's written down. The possibilities are endless.

A young violinist will find a well-defined path to teachers and orchestras. A young composer will not

Arguments rage. Some pupils prosper under the new freedoms; others simply use the school computer to do their 'composing' for them. And for serious students there may even come a time when the curriculum's lack of a thorough technical basis begins to impede the very creative process it was designed to free. According to Martin Butler, composer and lecturer at Sussex University, new university music students nowadays 'often show very little evidence of even rudimentary technical skills – there's no guarantee even via A-level, of musical literacy. The composer as we would have understood it ten years ago has become a very rare breed.'

Can you teach composing?

So how does composing get taught? Pupils beginning GCSE composition around the age of 14 need, says Phillip Flood, 'a tremendous stimulus. You've got to start from something that already exists – a rhythm, a bass line, a chord sequence – and work out from that.' Most pupils at this stage will be composing by ear and instinct rather than with any sort of acquired technique, and will tend to produce small, dramatic musical gestures rather than pieces developed and structured over long timespans – GCSE syllabuses typically ask for two or three contrasting pieces of a couple of minutes each, so the epic manner is not yet required (although consistency of ideas and logical developments are still prized by examiners). The starting points might be pictorial or narrative as much as purely musical, and pieces might get written down initially not in musical notation but as graphic symbols or verbal descriptions. As students progress, says Flood, 'the other aspects of the curriculum, listening and performance, hopefully begin to feed into their composing and start to give pupils an idea of the sort of music they want to write.' Many teachers will take pupils through a series of exercises, analysing and writing in different compositional styles: developing a motif, using ostinati, writing tonal and atonal music. Pupils might gain practical experience of notation, part-writing and instrumentation by writing pieces for one another, while the study of existing pieces may suggest solutions to just about any compositional problem (and, as Flood says, a benefit of the holistic approach is that 'you can take any piece of music that you might be working on with your instrumental teacher and turn it into a compositional project'). This is a start. A distinctive voice will be some distance away. Technical facility still needs to be worked on: no serious student can proceed without learning how to score for the different instruments, how to mix timbres, how to develop harmony, how to form larger structures – in short, to realise the full potential of their musical ideas. This will usually be the focus of post-18 study.

So where does all this leave the young composer? One problem is that although the current system is good at starting people off, it's less good at keeping them going. The lack of continuity between the composer-friendly GCSE and the composer-rather-less-friendly A-level is one alleged hurdle, as can be the lack of a sympathetic teacher, or indeed the general absence of opportunity full stop. Compared to performers of the same age, there are few channels down which aspiring young composers can progress. A gifted 14-year-old violinist will find a well defined network of teachers, orchestras, competitions waiting for him or her; a 14-year-old composer will not, though the BBC Young Musicians and BBC Symphony Orchestra Young Composers' Forum are

ACTION POINTS

● Improvisation, also on the GCSE syllabus, is one way into composition. Any piece you are performing can teach you something about composition

● SPNM runs a project to help pupils bridge the gap between GCSE and A-level. They also offer composing kits and a magazine for 16- to 19-year-olds, *Beat*

●Don't isolate yourself: join the SPNM, contact local composers, attend a summer school.

● The Incorporated Society of Musicians keeps a list of composition teachers

● Don't compose in a vacuum: who will play your piece? Seek out groups and orchestras

good examples of stimulating workshop events, in which selected composers can get advice on their work from distinguished masters of the craft. Still, research by the Society for the Promotion of New Music (SPNM) shows that teachers, often lacking the relevant skills themselves, tend to steer students away from composition after GCSE – as Flood says, 'it's still the area of the curriculum which frightens teachers the most'.

Essentially, ambitious young composers still face the same old problems – the difficulty of getting their pieces played, the lack of support, the sense of isolation. One important new initiative is the SPNM's 'Composing Beyond GCSE', a project which aims to help both teachers and pupils negotiate the difficult step up to

A-level (its *Beat* magazine and composition kits offer useful resource materials too). Summer holidays are a good time to make up for any deficiencies at school and a chance to mix with other aspiring composers. The Dartington International Summer School, for instance, is particularly strong on composition. But by and large, the best option is still to realise that if you want a thing doing, do it yourself. The important thing, Colin Riley says, is to get out into the world: 'The more you do, the better your chances. Join the SPNM, submit pieces, get in touch with local composers, find yourself a sympathetic teacher [the Incorporated Society of Musicians keeps a list of composition teachers]. Even activities which aren't obviously related to composing may lead to something that is. Maybe an orchestra you've been playing in will ask you for a piece; maybe some of its members will want to form a group to play new scores – the quicker you realise that, the quicker things will start happening. It's a good lesson to learn early on.'

Maybe this is not quite the image of a composer you had in mind. The portrait of the impoverished genius feverishly scrawling masterpieces in a garret is, says Martin Butler, one which 'has changed and should change'. Most would agree. Because a young person composes doesn't necessarily mean they're either (a) the new Mozart or (b) unwell. The urge to express oneself in sounds is, as Butler puts it, 'a very natural part of being a musician', but the fact of doing so shouldn't encourage either exaggerated hopes or fears. And although the actual writing itself is inevitably a solitary business, not everything composers do is so cut off from the world outside. What's increasingly emphasised is the idea of the composer as a (more-or-less) normal individual whose work has direct links with the community at large, who writes for specific people and places, and who's not afraid to go out and explain what they're trying to do. As composers become increasingly open to the world, so the world becomes a friendlier place for composers. Even so, the difficulties shouldn't be underestimated. Composing remains a tough proposition. Only a minority will succeed, and only an exceptional few will make a living out of it. There are, however, increasing opportunities, through educational and community work, to find a role, and to use that role as a springboard for one's own creative urges. Today's pupils are tomorrow's (better) teachers, and potentially those who will be writing the music which will fill the concert halls of the 21st century. If the Romantics succeeded briefly in shutting composers up in an ivory tower, the 20th century has taken them – and the act of composing itself – out and put them back in the mainstream. Which is where they always belonged. *Gavin Thomas*

See back of book for contact details

14. GCSE and A-level

A revolution in the classroom

WHAT DO WE MEAN when we opt to study 'music' at school? In the past it meant Western classical music from about 1400 to 1960. The few who took music O-level were those with five to ten years of one-to-one instrumental tuition behind them, theory exams, a second instrument and an understanding of music to which their classmates could never aspire. For the latter group this subject simply wasn't an option, but an irrelevant museum piece, which bore no relation to their experience of music on the radio, in the dance clubs or on their own keyboard or electric guitar.

So it was changed – radically. 'Music' now embraces pop, rock, folk and the music of other world cultures. The aim is for candidates to recognise how all these different genres work and to get well and truly stuck in, creating their own pieces, performing them, learning to improvise and making music as a group. And access is open: these candidates do not need to have been attending weekly lessons since the age of five. Some boards specifically state that the exam should be possible for those who have only received tuition in the classroom. Nevertheless, there has been a price to pay. When you expand a discipline this much you are bound to spread it more thinly.

The result is that music, perhaps above all other subjects, has become the focus of a heated ideological battle among educationalists. The introduction of the radical GCSE syllabus in the Eighties resulted in an explosion of interest in creative music-making among students. As David Murphy of Pimlico School, London, comments: 'Music used to be a very passive subject, you sat there and listened and absorbed information. Now it is much more active and creative and has become

14

very popular. The minority of students who used to take music to a high level in our school were isolated and ostracised by the other pupils. Now there are hundreds of students involved in practical music-making and the less advanced students appreciate the skill the others have when it comes to their own compositions being performed. It's transformed the department.'

Few would disagree that the new exams have had a tremendously positive effect in the majority of state schools. Children with no privileged background in music learning have been allowed free rein to make the sort of music they like best.

But there is another point of view, and one notably held by teachers at schools where a healthy level of entry was the norm and the standards of performing are traditionally high. At Pimlico, which boasts a special course, music specialists take GCSE at 14, and then spend the next two years preparing for A-level. At the famously academic St Paul's School for Girls the head of music, composer Derek Bourgeois, is not alone in ignoring Music GCSE entirely. 'I have devised my own pre-A-level course for those who wish to take it further. It covers all the ground. The music GCSE is simply a waste of time for our pupils.'

The new music exams have had a very positive effect in making music a more active subject and one accessible to more students

Teachers like Bourgeois feel that it doesn't get to grips with the fundamental basics of harmony, counterpoint and history. Self-expression is all very well but have pupils got the technical skills to master music writing? Easy access to effective computer programmes takes the drudgery out of scoring, but may also limit the imagination by offering cliched options. Paul McCartney is a good example of someone who has been handicapped by his lack of technical know-how: the idea for the *Liverpool Oratorio* was his own, but it ended up sounding very like the work of film composer Carl Davis, who had notated and orchestrated it. Subsequently, in his *Standing Stone* symphony, he called in no fewer than three top-level composers to help him make sense of what he wanted to hear. The anti-GCSE teachers would say that a budding McCartney is being let down by the system if he isn't taught the complex craft-skills of music. As Hugh Benham, chief examiner of the London-based Edexcel examining board and a former sixth-form music teacher notes, 'The trouble with the sort of pop music that many students want to write themselves is that it often has a very narrow range of material, and is therefore limiting.' Pimlico's David Murphy counters this tendency in his students by insisting that they all learn to identify and analyse historical styles in music, which feed into their compositions.

GCSE syllabus

Leaving aside minor regional board differences, the exam is basically divided into listening and appraising (30%), composing (30%), performing (30%), and, in general, one of a list of options, expanding any one of these areas (10%). The listening exam is generally broken down into musical perception, literacy (where you will notate the things you are hearing) and questions on set works. A typical list of set works would be this from the Edexcel board, 1998: Bernstein's *West Side Story*, six Chopin Preludes, Handel's *Messiah*, Haydn's London Symphony, Britten *Soirées musicales* and four songs from the pop group ELO. As well as pop and different world musics, you will be expected to identify different music examples in the Renaissance, Baroque, Classical, Romantic, Serialist and other modern styles. Composing and/or arranging will be judged submission of two, three or four pieces, of a combined duration of between two and ten minutes. The performing exam will involve playing solo or ensemble, or directing an ensemble, and some form of sight-reading. The voice counts as an instrument.

If you are post-Grade 4, you will sail through the performing part of the exam, but you would be well-advised to use the composition requirements to learn some basic harmony. You can ask your class or instrumental teacher on advice for further study (see Chapter 13). For the listening part of the exam you can never prepare enough. David Victor-Smith of Farnham Sixth Form College advises students who want to take music further to ensure they acquaint themselves with the broader picture of music history. He also encourages all students to sing regularly in a choir or choral group, since this will help them with the more advanced aural tests at A-level.

Preparing for A-level

Without music GCSE (Grade A or B) you will not be well-equipped for A-level unless you have followed a separate course of study, taken Grade 5 theory and are proficient on at least one instrument (to Grade 6-8 standard). But even with it the change of pace may come as a shock. At A-level, music is a much more academic subject. You will still be required to perform – Grade 6 is the minimum standard, Grade 8 for those who wish to take further performing options – and to compose. But added to this are further papers in aural perception, harmonic analysis, and historical periods. If you have only begun an instrument in your teens, have little experience of Associated Board aural and theory tests and have never sung in a choir, think carefully about what you want to achieve from the A-level before you start.

The first thing to find out, however, is whether or not your local

14

sixth form even offers music A-level: entry rates are traditionally low and classes small, which has made it uneconomic for some institutions to offer as a subject. Find out whether they have an arrangement with a nearby school, by which students can be farmed out for those lessons.

The core requirements are composing, performing and 'Listening and Appraising' papers, which involve listening to and answering questions on extracts (usually from an anthology with which you are familiar Edexcel has a list of 120 pieces). There will be musical dictation historical, harmonic and stylistic analysis for this part of the exam.

For some boards (Oxford and Cambridge) the emphasis is on learning harmonic and stylistic techniques through free composition. For others (Edexcel) the idea is to learn the techniques through imitation you will be given bars from a Haydn string quartet, a Romantic Lied or a Bach chorale and you must complete them using your knowledge of the writing styles. After this there are a variety of options, which means you can tailor it to your particular specialisms. You will be able to choose to do either more composing or performing, or a project, or practical musicianship skills such as harmonising chords, transposing, realising a figured bass or directing an ensemble.

There are also completely separate A-levels which emphasise one of the above (eg Edexcel's Performance, Music Theory, Music Technology). But be warned. If you have any thoughts of taking up music later at a conservatoire or university, your music A-level must have covered a large range of aural perception, analysis, harmony, compositional styles and historical periods.

The many different regional boards are currently merging into just three (Edexcel, AQA, OCR), and it will depend on where you are which syllabus you follow. But it is worth studying them carefully with your music teacher so that you can see just which options would be best for you. If you know you are not going to be studying music later on, then the performing exam – sometimes called Music Supplementary or Practical Music – may be a good one for you to take. You may be able to complete it in one year, so giving yourself a fourth A-level. If you have never excelled in performing, then the Music Theoretical may suit you better. For those who are sure that they want to be involved in sound engineering, recording, producing, or music industry generally, Music Technology deals with MIDI, sequencing, 24-track recording and electroacoustic composition. But this is only an option in schools with a highly-equipped studio and you could be at a real disadvantage if your music department is trying to make do with old or unsophisticated equipment. As with all courses, check on which vocational or degree courses now recognise this A-level. There is such a diversity of post-18 courses now that you should be prepared for some hefty research.

The Future: AS, A2, NBTEC, GNVQ

If A-level is still some way off for you, the above points may not apply, because after the year 2001 the entire A-level system is going to be overhauled, much in the way O-levels were. In the light of the Dearing Report, plans are now afoot to make a smoother learning curve between GCSE and A-level. The Report's aims were to maintain the standard of excellence set by high A-level grades, while providing a way in which more 16-plus candidates could follow the subject on logically from their GCSE. By the year 2002 there will probably be two exams, one for the first year of Sixth Form called the Subsidiary A-level and one for the second called A2. There will be a total of six modules, three in each year, which will be examined on a module-by-module basis. This has partly been suggested as a way of retaining more students into the Sixth Form and partly to prevent a too leisurely start in that first year.

The proposed new system is being welcomed by teachers who feel there is now a gap between GCSE and A-level which the O-level used to fill. The AS may stand as an equivalent to the Scottish Higher exam, which, taken at 17, currently follows a fairly stringent syllabus, including the recognition of many different historical musical styles, performance, improvisation, musical dictations of fairly complex works, a working knowledge of four-part harmony and a performance level on two instruments equivalent to Grade 4.

For the less academic post-GCSE candidates, the GNVQ route is an increasingly viable alternative. Although there is no one exam entitled 'music' there are several being developed under the Arts and Entertainment umbrella, such as the GNVQ in 'Performing Arts and the Entertainment Industries'. GNVQs are vocational qualifications which test you on competencies rather than knowledge, such as business skills, keyboard skills and performing skills. The BTEC exams, in Popular

ACTION POINTS

● GCSE has made music a more accessible subject to more pupils, embracing a range of cultures and musical styles

● Students wishing to pursue music after GCSE should widen their listening and join a choir

● GCSE students who have done free composition should know that some A-levels require them to imitate historical styles instead

● Familiarity with composing software is useful for GCSE

● You can select options at A-level to fit your skills, but make sure you aren't jeopardising university entrance by failing to cover fundamental areas

14

Music, Music Technology and Performing Arts are currently being piloted in a number of schools which have the resources and facilities to do them. Students who aim to do an HND or to go to one of the institutions which run courses in rock music, music technology and arts management (eg Salford, Liverpool Hope, De Montfort University) would be well-placed with this qualification under their belts. But you would have to be an exceptional candidate to persuade most universities that these form the equivalent of a music A-level. *Helen Wallace*

For details of examination boards, see listing at back of book

15. Sixth-form strategy

Mapping a path for the future

OF THE MANY fine reasons for choosing music as your course of study after school, only one has the ring of utter, unanswerable soundness: that you have to. Music is not what you do, but who you are. By the age of 17 some people have already made their commitment to the long adventure of training and discovery. For others, the moment to ask the big question comes in the final year of school. It is a question about yourself, not about your qualifications.

Singers, for instance, will develop their full physical potential in their twenties, and the opera world has plenty of late starters. Instrumentalists, in contrast, have to be better than proficient; it's already too late to make a pianist's or a violinist's fingers do what they have to do unless the body has been well worked on since childhood. Then again, creative music-making is a rule-free zone where no amount of practice can ignite the vital spark but combustion might occur at any age. For every Mozart there is a Bruckner. Sometimes it takes exposure to a different musical tradition from the one you started in – a flair for improvising can go very frustrated in post-Baroque Europe. It's also possible to pursue music when you know your limits and can live with them, as long as you would die if you had to do anything else. You will join an expanding universe of music-linked professions, from teaching to management, and escape one of the most competitive milieux of all.

Your decision now, which may look like a career choice, is really something more strategic. The majority of people who go into higher musical education end up earning their living in another field. Those who become full-time professional performers are a minority of a minority. It is absolutely essential to face this hard fact, because in the

15

past music students have been encouraged to be star-struck until it was too late. For a long time the teaching institutions did not give them realistic perspectives. These institutions were increasingly criticised within the musical world for failing to relate to the way that world was changing. Frankly, the really special musicians will have emerged before the age of 17, so what can music college offer the rest? Many have now begun to realise their responsibilities and offer new, exciting alternatives to the old-fashioned four years of technical self-improvement.

The music world is ruthlessly competitive; if you can't face it do something else and keep music for fun

Remember too that music studied at full stretch is as good a mind-former as mathematics or philosophy and you can move smoothly into many more general careers by way of appropriate courses after you graduate. Wise students know this all along. Unfortunately the world is also full of embittered musicians who cannot come to terms with failing to reach the unrealistic goals they were misled into believing at the outset. If you couldn't take the disappointment, do something else for a living and you will be able to keep the music for fun, which it won't be if you feel sour about it.

Having decided to go ahead, you come to some basic decisions about different kinds of education. There are several alternatives to the obvious choices, some less publicised, which, for the right people, are shrewd options.

Conservatoires

Traditionally, if you wanted to study a classical instrument to professional standards of performance you went to a conservatoire rather than university. Broadly the distinction is still true, though the options are more varied nowadays and you can end up in courses oriented towards teaching, community work and more besides. The central experience is one-to-one teaching on your principal instrument (or your voice) by a distinguished practitioner. Around that you can assemble a variety of ensemble performances, specialisms, theoretical and historical study and, increasingly, preparation for a wider range of musical employment.

Because of the long hours of solitary practice, you need a good strain of self-sufficiency in your nature if you are going to make the best of it. This applies particularly to London conservatoires where you may be living for some of your time a long way from the centre of town and can feel isolated. If you have been able to get well past Grade 8 standard with a smattering of public performances and good orchestra experience without depending on your family to kick you into doing some practice, then you probably have what it takes.

University

This is the usual option for people who want to deepen their knowledge in order to teach, research, stretch the mind while enriching the spirit, or simply for love of it. Some universities have become the choice of composers, others develop a reputation for practicality, thoroughness or tradition. Individual teachers attract students because of their intellectual perspective. Above all – and a prime reason for reading the small print in reference books and prospectuses – there is a range of individual specialities from the challenging to the quirky. And remember that in certain universities there will be more opportunities to make music than in the conservatoires.

Socially universities are more straightforward than conservatoires and you will meet people with a quite different range of professional and intellectual leanings. Special-interest societies exist to draw the most dedicated loners and nutters out of their shells. Everything from chess to synchronised swimming will have a fan somewhere.

Other higher education

Apart from the biggest conservatoires there are several colleges of music that offer the same kind of principal-instrument studies and often have more practical leanings. They will not usually be top choice for performing high-fliers, but some of them are a very attractive option if, say, you want to go into studio work or pursue electronic instruments. Taken together they offer a great diversity of music from down-to-earth commercial subjects to hard-to-find world music genres.

If you already know you want to teach in a school there is another option besides taking a music degree followed by a postgraduate teaching qualification. This is to take an undergraduate teaching course at a college of higher education with a strong music department. One difference is that usually you need to decide the age range you want to teach at the outset and most of these courses cater for primary and middle-school levels. For primary age ranges you train to teach a full range of subjects, not just music. A recent complication at this level is that the national curriculum no longer holds music to be compulsory, so that as things stand you will find when you come to look for a job that some schools take music more seriously than others. According to your attitude that could be a challenge to relish, or a deeply depressing experience. The situation is still controversial and further change is not beyond all possibility if the present ruling proves as unpopular in the classroom as it is with musicians.

Universities are the usual option for those who want to teach or research and have a wide range of individual specialities

15

The cunning option (or hedging your bets)

Musical performance is such an insecure profession that some people approach it with a built-in insurance policy. One ploy is to follow your conservatoire years with a training in straightforward office skills, whether in computers or in elements of accountancy. That way you are equipped for temporary work at times when you are 'resting' and can garner the beginnings of experience that may let you turn later towards a business career. But what about reversing the order? If you are patient enough to hold off for a year, or if the gap is forced on you, then you may find that you go to your college or university better able to supplement your income than most of your contemporaries.

Performers can also choose, instead of a conservatoire, to go to a university which has a large and active musical life open to all students. You do not have to read music and can give yourself two full-scale career options. The trick is to keep your lessons going with a teacher you trust and that depends on who is teaching you. This could be more expensive or demanding on time. Should you get into Oxford or Cambridge in any subject, you will be able to spend as much of your free time as you want making music with other people. The networking here is as good as it is at a conservatoire and better in church music and early music. They are still places where your next-door neighbour may be the future head of Radio 3. John Eliot Gardiner, Richard Hickox, Roger Norrington, Thomas Adès, Andrew Davis and Nicholas Snowman are all Cambridge graduates.

Most large universities will have plenty of music going on, but you need to make careful inquiries about the quality, just as you would about the music department. The positive side to doing it this way is that you will probably gain a wider experience of ensembles of many kinds, informal as much as formal, and become more confident. When it comes to the crunch, professional auditions are about how you play on the day, not what it says in your CV. But it's riskier this way and the option is best for people who care more about music than whether they make their living from it.

Robert Maycock

ACTION POINTS

- Only a tiny number of musicians become professional performers, but there is a huge range of other options

- Teaching institutions are now more realistic about this and offer courses to equip students

- Conservatoires still put emphasis on technical excellence

- Universities have a broader intake and often more opportunities for informal music-making

- Remember you will have to take out a student loan, though there may be scholarships and awards. Fees are approx. £1,000 per year

16. Conservatoires and music colleges

Navigating in a fast-changing world

BRITAIN HAS SOME of the most famous conservatoires in the world which, at their best, have set world-class standards of adaptable, quick-thinking musicianship. They are now at a fascinating stage of transition. Once seen as secure bastions of European musical tradition, they have entered on a gradual, inexorable process of change. To understand why, you need to observe the way the musical world is changing around them. Many of the issues are reported prominently in the media, at least on the level of dwindling orchestral audiences, overpriced opera tickets and the ever-present fear of cuts in funding. Below this rather alarmist surface, musicians' lives have been quietly transforming themselves. A spectrum of musical careers has opened up that previous generations never knew and the challenge for the conservatoires has been to prepare their students for what is out there now.

The growth area in Britain's classical music over the last decade has been in work with the community and the key to it is an attitude of sharing skills. All the main performing organisations have developed extensive community and education programmes which can run from creative workshops in schools to performance projects with long-term prisoners. They employ specialist leaders and animateurs, not only to plan and run sessions like these, but to train members of the orchestra or company in doing some of the work themselves. Increasingly, smaller and newer music groups find that they are in demand for the same reasons. Many of the new musical opportunities are on a local scale. In cities and towns around Britain, visiting and resident musicians are being asked not just to play concerts but to work with selected

16

pupils from schools and with other community groups. In the longer term musicians can take up residencies, committing regular amounts of time to the area and becoming an integral part of its musical life.

There are plenty of other signs of growth. Take contemporary music: what used to be a matter of a few big commissions for successful composers has exploded into burgeoning creativity spread through a bewildering variety of places. Highly trained, experienced musicians are working live or as DJs on the fast-moving club scene. The line between an arcane studio experiment and the next dance style is thin and rapidly crossed. Asian music is on the rise at all levels from pop charts to classical concerts. Jazz is a college subject in its own right and has Arts Council budgets for promoters (see Chapter 11). New television channels need music for programmes and commercial breaks and so does the currently successful British film industry. A lot of younger musicians move easily between several of these musical areas and have a much more varied life than the orchestral players of earlier generations.

In short, the death-of-music pundits have got it wrong. What has happened is that the familiar world of orchestras, operas and recitals has had to condense for economic reasons. Fewer new recordings need to be made of familiar repertoire and audiences are so spoilt for choice that they want more from a live event than just another performance of a well-known piece. But as this has happened, other kinds of music have sprung up to absorb the same energy and skill.

At first it was all too fast for the profession and for the conservatoires to adapt to. Now, each year sees more new courses and modules designed to prepare students for a new slice of the exciting life that is out there for them, if only somebody can show them how to reach it.

Refining the choice

This is the background to have in mind when you are reading the prospectus of a conservatoire. All of them place the main tradition of Western classical music at the centre. For years they worked on the principle that their job was done when the musician was fully formed, usually as a soloist. Now they accept that expensive specialised training in music, like any other field, needs to give some economic return. For the potential student it adds a dimension to deciding which one will suit best. As well as trying to find which will have the best teacher for you, there is now a chance of steering your future life in a number of different directions.

The question of teaching as a career often seems to be a vexed one among conservatoire students. It shouldn't be; teaching is really part of ll professionals' futures. Most of them will choose or be asked to give one-to-one lessons at some point and orchestral and ensemble players increasingly have to take part in school and community projects. But in the past those who took specific teachers' courses used to be looked on as the non-star performers, for all that their work would make greater intellectual demands. Even now, with fierce competition to get into the main college orchestra and other prestige ensembles, those who turn to teaching have to resist an attitude that seems to be ingrained in the fabric of the institutions. For some it is a factor that may tip the balance towards university instead. (Other teaching options are covered in Chapters 17 and 18.) Others will thrive on the many signs of improvement. As more people emerge from an experience of courses like the Guildhall's Performance and Communication Skills (part of its degree course), so they learn to respect the particular gifts and skills that are needed for this kind of work. Moving on to specialise in it is a positive choice to exercise abilities that the high-flying performers often simply do not possess.

Whatever your line of study, there are a number of basic principles to follow in fining down your choice. Make sure you get the most up-to-date prospectus. It may sound obvious, but people do end up borrowing old ones from friends and expecting to find teachers who no longer work at that conservatoire. While the overall policy may not change overnight, new courses or modules are always coming in. Learn to read between the lines. It is often a question of seeing what the prospectus leaves out and you can do that more easily if you have several.

The same goes for courses. Prospectuses don't tell you about possibly more interesting options elsewhere. Here the *Music Education Yearbook* is invaluable for getting a bird's eye view of course details. When you know what you are looking for, try to talk to people who have been there and, if possible, visit the place. If you have been to Saturday junior departments at any of the conservatoires you will know what the building is like, but the life is quite different during the week. You will read lists of musicians who teach there and you need to judge who will

---

ACTION POINTS

● British conservatoires are in a stage of transition as they adapt to a new range of musical careers

● The main growth area in classical music is in community work, with musicians in demand to organise workshops and work with the young or disadvantaged

● Foundation courses are a good way to see if conservatoire life suits you before it's too late to apply to university

● Make sure you are aware of the ever increasing range of specialist courses and modules

16

be best for you. This is easier if you have a chance to talk it through with some current students. You may be able to arrange a consultation lesson with a teacher. The new idea of foundation courses is a great way of trying out the life, if it fits in with your school work: it means you attend part-time while you are doing your A-level studies and can judge whether the regime will suit you before it is too late to apply to university instead. Plan ahead and ask whether the conservatoire is likely to have a scheme like this in the year you would want it. Remember that most music colleges have four-year courses, with options to stay on for further postgraduate courses afterwards.

The conservatoires (in alphabetical order)

Birmingham Conservatoire: the most recent to become a full-scale conservatoire and still growing. It offers Bachelor degrees in music (BMus) for performance or composition and theory workshops with improvisation/composition links. All first years include world music. Early, jazz and community music specialisms are possible, plus wide-ranging creative studies. The City of Birmingham Symphony Orchestra is a neighbour and has strong links.

Guildhall School of Music and Drama, London: part of Barbican complex. It has an integrated approach with all students spending time on jazz/improvisation, conducting and studio music and performance and communications skills – GSMD pioneered this community-oriented course. Students can be involved with postgraduate activities in, for example, early music and opera – a particular strength. The post-graduate Music Therapy course was pioneered here. Composition is high-profiled.

Leeds College of Music: a new purpose-built premises. It offers a Specialist Jazz Studies Bachelor of Arts (BA) as well as Bachelor of Performing Arts (Music). Outward-looking elements include popular music, Indian music (included in the foundation programme) technology/instument repair, music and media. There are computer and recording studios and a jazz/popular archive.

London College of Music and Media: relocated from city centre to Ealing, continues a career-oriented approach with diplomas in popular music performance and music technology. BMus (Performance) also gives traditional training a contemporary emphasis. Composition includes film/TV, theatre and new media options.

Royal Academy of Music, London: developed an international outlook in staff and student intake while maintaining British teaching traditions. Performance excellence is the aim, but it now cultivates a reciprocal link with King's College (London University) to widen teachng and support resources. Jazz and commercial music are available as principal study subjects, good orchestral reputation, contemporary music festivals, individual flexibility in make-up of courses.

Royal College of Music, London: composing tradition (from Vaughan Williams, Britten onwards) continues alongside main emphasis on performance. Balance of practical and academic work decided after first year. Nowadays well researched and aware of career options. Teaching relationships with well-known professional groups. Student ensembles include big band and early music group. Conducting opportunities. Famous library. Orchestral studies postgrad year is extremely practical.

Royal Northern College of Music, Manchester: highly visible on musical scene thanks to the use of performing spaces for outside promotions, plus its own international cello festival. It has much contact with the wider profession and good performing opportunities. The wind orchestra is of professional standard. There is a flexible course structure after the first year with academic principal study an option. It has produced some well-known composition graduates.

Royal Scottish Academy of Music and Drama, Glasgow: at the heart of the nation's musical life and has links with Royal Scottish National Orchestra, Scottish Opera and (via its own studio) TV. It is strong in new and traditional music: a BA (Scottish Music) as well as Musical Studies and Performance degrees. Also offers Bachelor of Education. Support studies aim to be practical and include career management.

Trinity College of Music, London: has become employment-conscious with its BMus 'Music Plus' degree which is performance-based but takes a broad approach to career possibilities including contacts with music-business employers. 'Musicianship' includes improvising and historical/theoretical subjects are integrated from the start. Modular choices open up later. Undergraduate degrees are validated by Westminster University.

Welsh College of Music and Drama, Cardiff: a national-capital conservatoire that takes advantage of the presence of arts institutions including Welsh National Opera and the BBC National Orchestra of Wales. Three-year BA and Diploma courses are performance-oriented (the latter more so). There are music technology facilities with several studios including recording and TV. *RM*

See back of book for contact details

16

17. Choosing a degree course

The pros and cons of university life

AT A UNIVERSITY music department the rhythm of life is quite different from a conservatoire (see Chapter 16). The level of performing skills is more mixed and mental virtuosity counts for more than technical. You spend more time in the department itself and the atmosphere, although challenging, is more relaxed and less competitive. Probably your sense of a future career is going to be formed as you go along, unless you already have outstanding flair or commitment in a specific musical field.

Those with ambitions to teach will know that they have to obtain a postgraduate teaching qualification later and that, for the time being, breadth of musical experience is a good idea.

If you want to treat music as a formative discipline rather than your direct source of employment, you will have access to the main careers services of the university and be in a position to take guidance in many postgraduate options. To make the most effective choice of university, however, you need to approach the prospect with some idea of your preferences. If you want a broad general grounding in music, some universities are simply better equipped than others.

The variety of more specialised possibilities is bewilderingly large. As with conservatoires, you need to equip yourself with as much information as possible: reference books first, then a department prospectus for every place that interests you. If you want to check further on your personal interests, get the details of postgraduate courses. These will often tell you what research interests are being pursued and, by implication, what the staff know about. Postgraduates may take an informal part in the teaching and can be a valuable source of expertise and advice.

The latent composer

Assuming you have settled the basics like how far away from home you want to live, staff and resources are the key. You will see some well-known names, particularly composers, on the list. The really effective ones will be known for attracting like-minded spirits to study with them. Cambridge (Alexander Goehr, Robin Holloway, Hugh Wood), Manchester (John Casken, Geoffrey Poole), Edinburgh (Nigel Osborne) and Sussex (Michael Finnissy, Jonathan Harvey) have the highest profile for composers in the Western classical tradition, although they are only three among many. The more maverick Gavin Bryars sets the tone at Leicester University, for example. If you are out of sorts with present-day contemporary classsical music they may be completely wrong for you. Do not assume that because you admire a composer's work he or she will necessarily be a rewarding teacher. Some composers are anything but open-minded towards other ways of making music, even when their own seems quite eclectic, while others show a patience and generosity of spirit that you would never guess from what they write.

A university can offer students the opportunity to listen, absorb and experiment without having to decide on a career

If you are serious about creative study at university, it's worth having a detailed discussion with somebody who can see your side of the picture as well as knowing the scene – one of your teachers should be able to come up with a contact. Alternatively you can plunge in anyway and see how you get on. There is plenty of time to move on when you have graduated, university having offered a marvellous opportunity to listen, absorb, try things out either by performing or writing scores for other people, without feeling forced to declare your full hand. Composers David and Colin Matthews, for instance, studied other subjects at university.

Special interests

Finding out who's who around the universities can also reveal where there might be postgraduate interest in a particular topic. For instance, avid Schubertians will know that the professor at Hull is Brian Newbould, who has prepared performing versions of Schubert's various unfinished symphonies and written the definitive biography. The musician who did a similar service for an incomplete Debussy opera, Richard Langham Smith, is on the staff at Exeter, where Chopin specialist Jim Samson also teaches; Czech expert Jan Smaczny is at Queen's University, Belfast; and Barry Cooper, author of an exhaustive study of Beethoven's sketch books, is at Manchester. Fauré expert Robert Orledge is at Liverpool and so forth. For most undergraduates,

17

however, the important factors will be more general: facilities, breadth of coverage, specific courses.

Gauging the temperature

As with conservatoires you must be prepared to read between the lines about facilities. The institution that boasts of its fine electroacoustic studio will not go out of its way to tell you whether it is irritatingly short of normal practice rooms, so you may need to ask around. However, you can be fairly certain that if a department takes enough pride in one or another aspect to publicise it prominently, that opinion will be shared elsewhere. One example is electronic and studio music. The founding activists in Britain's Sonic Arts Network made their way through the studios at City University, London, and Birmingham. These departments won their reputations early and have long traditions of developing the medium. More studios, at the University of East Anglia and York, for instance, have now sprung up – the Sonic Arts organisation can give you details which will be a useful supplement to what the universities provide. In professional recording techniques, the University of Surrey has a well-known four-year Tonmeister Bachelor of Music course which combines an academic music training with detailed technical tuition.

Approaches to the formal intellectual elements of music education – history, analysis, techniques such as orchestration – vary enormously, even from individual to individual within a department. Durham and Oxford are sought after for their long traditions of laying down a solid foundation, but plenty of other universities cover the ground well and, as lecturers move from one to another during their careers, the scene is constantly developing. For most people, though, the key question is what kinds of music are on offer. The answers are also good indicators of whether the department is traditional, progressive, broad-minded, and so on. Here are some more possibilities, mentioned as appetite-whetters, not as a listing or a recommendation:

City University, London, takes a global perspective on musical history and music in cultural life.

Durham combines strength in ethnomusicology and thoroughness in the Western tradition.

Goldsmiths' College, London, has a history of radicalism, a commitment to adult education and an orchestral studies course.

Huddersfield University is the home of the annual Festival of Contemporary Music, at which time it becomes a major international networking centre.

Keele has a track record in American music with specialist David Nicholls. The psychology department has links with music.

King's College, London, has developed links with the Royal Academy of Music and undergraduates take their music lessons there.

Leeds has a BMus for advanced performers which includes a year at a conservatoire abroad.

Oxford and **Cambridge** have uniquely strong choral traditions with a system of college chapels and choral scholarships

Queen's University, Belfast, hosts major festivals in new and early music and has the Ulster Orchestra as next-door neighbours who teach.

Salford is a big centre for all kinds of popular and band music, in theory and practice.

The School of Oriental and African Studies, London, has an option which includes study of Western music at King's College.

Surrey has a well-established Tonmeister course for recording engineers.

York combines expertise in contemporary music with a well-informed approach to world classical traditions. They have a continuous assessment approach and strong emphasis on performance.

Other choices

There is a vestigial amount of prejudice in some quarters about old and new universities – the ones that used to be polytechnics. This should be resisted because some of the new ones are on the ball about relating to the contemporary musical world. Anglia, formerly Cambridge Polytechnic, was well known for its music department and its jazz courses 30 years ago. Elsewhere there is a will to engage with the areas that actually generate work. One example is the University of Northumbria at Newcastle, which specifically offers vocational training in music in the community, focused on popular music with a full range of theoretical and practical work.

The same goes for the colleges of higher education. They include such respected centres as Christ Church College in Canterbury, the Colchester Institute, Dartington College of Arts and Liverpool Hope University College. Colchester, for instance, has a feet-on-the-ground approach that combines sound traditional training with more vocational options, including business studies and music for people with special needs. It also has two foundation courses (see Chapter 16 for an explanation of the term) designed to prepare students for university, conservatoire and college entry – one of them specialising in popular music. Christ Church has some high-powered visiting teachers and consultants, a strong performance basis and plenty of practical subjects. You can combine music here with anything from tourism to sports science. However, the standard of playing would not be nearly as high as at conservatoires or even Oxbridge.

17

Christ Church is also one of the leading colleges that train teachers. The once familiar Bachelor of Education degree is now being replaced by the BA Qualified Teacher Status (QTS) as your passport into acceptance for full-time school work. A few universities also offer undergraduate QTS courses. Once again there is a range of special interests, although diversity of musical coverage would seem to be the best preparation for teaching children in different social environments.

Combined honours degrees in general are a case for argument. They are available at quite a number of universities and colleges and involve dividing your time between two quite separate departments with their own ways of doing things. Some combinations make good practical sense if you are aiming to work in a particular line – music and a foreign language, music and media studies, music and education, for instance. The case against is that they leave you underexposed in the music itself and may narrow your options rather than broadening them.

Passing muster

When you apply to a conservatoire the crunch encounter is the audition. For universities and colleges of higher education, at least those that do not make decisions entirely on paper, it is the interview – and A-level grades. While the university is sizing you up, you should remember that the process is mutual and this is your opportunity to ask questions too. A check-list can include any of the following: Who will be assessing my work and what are their criteria? How do they deal with musical theory – on paper, at the keyboard, by improvisation? Are there professional musicians-in-residence? How much performance is organised through the department? If, when you leave, you have a hunch that the place isn't right for you, listen to your doubts and act on your conclusions. You can spend three years regretting the wrong decision, whereas a little more time pursuing another option might give you just the answer you are looking for. *Robert Maycock*

See back of book for contact details

ACTION POINTS

● At university performing skills are more mixed and mental virtuosity matters more than technical

● Find out details of postgraduate courses: this will give you an idea of teacher specialisms in a given university

● Staff and resources are key factors to consider once you've identified a suitable course

● Combined degrees make sense for certain careers but can limit your musical experience

● If you are invited for interview always quiz the interviewers about assessment criteria, musicians-in-residence, performance opportunities, etc

18. External diplomas

Perfecting performance and honing teaching skills

SO YOU HAVE decided not to go to a music conservatoire; perhaps you are not going to study music at university or polytechnic either. You might have opted for an astro-physics or law degree, but one thing's certain: you've got Grade 8 stowed away, and you don't want to let your playing skills slump into sloppiness. Every year thousands of musicians in similar circumstances set their adrenalin pumping once more and focus their performance skills by taking an external diploma with one of several conservatoires or a distinguished examination board such as the Associated Board of the Royal Schools of Music or Trinity College, London.

Maybe you want to have the option of doing private teaching or working as a peripatetic part-time teacher for a local authority. You could have a handful of pupils already but would like some letters after your name for personal confidence or kudos. Whatever your scenario, there is a wealth of post-Grade 8 exams and diplomas out there.

For performance diplomas, the good news is that opportunities are widening. Alongside the more obvious instrumental awards lie ones for gospel music, music theatre and drum kit. And there's a growing trend towards all-encompassing disciplines such as early music or jazz. If instrumental or vocal skills aren't your particular forte, then you could go for composition, bandmastership or other forms of conducting.

Recently, the greatest and in my eyes most welcome changes, in terms of exam content and preparation, are those external diplomas for instrumental and vocal teaching. Requirements have deepened with the accent on teaching methods and hands-on experience rather than performance. The results are much more tuned-in to the practicalities

18

of being a teacher. Instigating the changes, however, takes time as the current state of flux indicates: Birmingham Conservatoire is revising its teaching diploma and hopes to have one up and running in 1999/2000; the Royal College of Music completely withdrew its external teaching diploma in 1997 and the Guildhall School is substantially revising its teaching licentiate with a view to announcing a course in 1999. Three years ago the Associated Board introduced a new and widely admired certificate of teaching on top of its existing teaching licentiate; it's a part-time, workshop-oriented professional development course aimed at teachers currently practising or music graduates who want to teach.

External diplomas for music teachers place more emphasis on teaching methods and experience than performance

At last, examination boards are addressing the fact that, in the words of Nicholas King, chief examiner of music at Trinity College, London, 'It's inevitable but regrettable that the best performers don't necessarily make the best teachers. To find someone that's excellent in both is quite rare.'

If you are seriously planning to take on instrumental teaching as a career, however, be warned: external teaching diploma qualifications from any college are no longer accepted by the Department for Education and Employment for Qualified Teacher Status. This means that although you can still be employed by a local authority to work in schools and colleges, you will have to accept a lower rate of pay and it's usually more difficult for you to find full-time employment than someone who has undertaken an internal course followed by a year of training for a Postgraduate Certificate in Education (PGCE), or completed a Bachelor of Education degree (see Chapter 17).

Whether you're keen or simply not sure of the nitty-gritty demanded by the various diplomas, a look at a few of the finer points may be of assistance. This chapter will concentrate on the more popular performance and teaching associates and licentiates. (More advanced Fellowships can also be obtained from the colleges or boards mentioned.) Specialist colleges such as the Royal College of Organists are well worth investi-

---

ACTION POINTS

● External diplomas are a good way to focus performance skills if you are not at a music college

● There is a widening range of diplomas in fields from bandmastership to gospel music

● Teaching diplomas are now more tuned to the practicalities of one-to-one tuition

● Check which qualifications are accepted by the government for Qualified Teacher Status

● There are stepping stones to a diploma which you may need to take first, such as advanced certificates

gating if that's your particular field.

If you don't feel confident about leaping into a professional diploma straight away, there are several options which can form stepping stones. Quite often these certificates are necessary pre-requisites for the professional exams anyway. For instance, you must pass the Royal Schools of Music's Advanced Certificate before applying for the board's Performance or Teaching licentiates; similarly, the associate diplomas offered by Trinity College, London, and London College of Music which test all-round performance skills equivalent to a student at the end of their first year at music college, have to have been passed before going on to either of their licentiate awards. For Trinity College, an additional two-hour written diploma has to be taken; the London College is unique in providing a junior teaching diploma, the associate teaching, for 15-year-olds and over; the London College also offers a lower-level Advanced Performance Certificate, a recital-only exam in which you are expected to be of conservatoire entry standard. When it comes to the crunch, it's worth phoning around to check out syllabuses more thoroughly – find out what's available, whether you're exempt from certain written papers or qualifying exams, how often exams are held per year and whether they are held in a convenient local centre. Remember that you always have to provide your own accompanist.

Professional performance diplomas

The licentiate of the **Guildhall School of Music and Drama** solely examines your recital skills, so much so that the public are allowed to come in and listen (it's the only one of its kind). Communication is important and marks are awarded for the way you engage the audience. You don't have to write your own programme notes but are encouraged to introduce the pieces. You're free to choose your own well-balanced programme, but it has to be approved. It is expected that all successful candidates would be taken seriously in a professional audition. (The jazz diploma involves improvisation, group sessions and a written paper.) The fee is £200.

The **London College of Music** is the only college to present both a performers' diploma and a performers' recital diploma. Neither have a written paper. The first (for which you have to have an associate-level pass prior to entering) involves a 45-minute practical exam with recital and sight-reading. Credit is given to candidates who perform from memory. For the recital diploma there are no prerequisites for entrance, the whole performance must be carried out from memory and there is no sight-reading. Fees for both are £125.

The **Royal College of Music** has no licentiate, but a £125 associate

18

diploma instead. The norm is a 50-minute recital chosen from a list of recommended pieces, plus sight-reading. Singers and pianists have to perform from memory; other instrumentalists should play at least one piece without music. For Early Music candidates, the ARCM can be carried out on one instrument or voice, or two instruments; the recital is shorter but there's a *viva voce* too.

The **Royal Schools of Music** licentiate is unusual in that it comprises two written papers (there are some exemptions): one harmony, the other a general history of music. Your recital (40 minutes) should be given from memory and you have to write your own programme notes. There's a discussion of chosen works and repertoire questions. The fee is £213 (£63 for the written; £150 for the practical).

At **Trinity College, London**, the licentiate involves a 40-minute recital of one prescribed work (there is rarely a choice) and two others from a selected list, plus sight-reading. You don't have to write programme notes, but the college encourages introducing the works. Early music diplomas were introduced in 1997 and have slightly different requirements. The fee is £95.

Teaching diplomas (instrumental or vocal)

These all demand qualifications at associate or equivalent level (ie one licentiate level) prior to applying, except the Associated Board's certificate of teaching.

The licentiate of the **London College of Music** comprises a two-part exam with quite some weight on performance. Section One involves two written papers covering the theory and history of music, the principles of teaching and specifics to your instrument. Section Two is a 50-minute practical exam, including recital, sight-reading, scales, a *viva voce* on principles of teaching, and you might have to give a demonstration lesson. No teaching experience is stipulated, although it's encouraged. There is a £150 fee.

The two written papers of Part One of the licentiate of the **Royal Schools of Music** consist of harmony and the history of music. Part Two involves three sections. The first requires case studies of three pupils that you've taught for six months and the shadowing of an experienced teacher for six months. The second is a three-hour written paper on the art of teaching and the third a one-hour practical exam with recital, sight-reading on chosen instrument and piano; discussion on your case studies and performance of a prepared keyboard accompaniment. The fee is £213.

At **Trinity College, London**, emphasis is placed on practical demonstrations of teaching methods rather than on the demanding recital expectations of those above. Part One is a two-hour written paper covering the principles of teaching. Part Two, rather unusually, involves a 50-minute practical element with no recital or mainstream sight-reading tests, but you are expected to perform various tasks relating to practical teaching skills. There's a five-part structure and all sections have to be passed. You don't have to shadow a teacher or practise teaching yourself, although the experience would obviously help. The college has introduced diplomas for teaching instrumental families to serve the demands of today's peripatetic teacher. The fee is £105 (£84 for the practical and £21 for the written).

Additionally, Trinity offers Certificate, Associate and Licentiate diplomas in Music Education. Around 1,000 active teachers are registered to pursue studies to advance their own professional development by attending courses organised by the College and other professional bodies, and by completing a practical examination which tests skills in performance, composition and improvisation.

Three years ago, the **Associated Board of the Royal Schools of Music** introduced a one-year, part-time professional development course or certificate of teaching, which incorporates 13 days of study, teaching skills and techniques with a mentor, assessment of pupils and curriculum development. It's aimed at music students or established music teachers and is open access (you have to be 21 or, for singers, 25), although you must have taught at least three pupils per week for a year. There are about 100 hours of tuition in all and the course is held in centres all round the country for a fee of £1,595.
Kate Sherriff

See back of book for contact details

18

What next?

'Music doesn't just happen, it is what we make it, and what we make *of* it. People think through music, decide who they are through it, express themselves through it.'
Nicholas Cook

THERE ARE AS many different musical experiences as there are people; and just as there is no one music, there is no one ultimate goal to which everyone must aspire. Because of the enormous technical ability required of musicians, progress can become as linearly competitive as sport. And because of the exceptional level of originality and intellect required of a 'great' composer, we sometimes fail to appreciate what is being achieved under our noses.

We cannot all be Beethovens or Barenboims, but it's amazing how many parents and children feel they have failed if their 10-15 years of study does not result in an engagement at the Proms, or on the BBC Young Musicians competition, at the very least. How often have I heard the parental cry, 'When are you going to play your clarinet/cello/piano again?'. How betrayed one parent felt when her son, a talented cellist, won a place at music college and promptly took up the sitar. How much simpler it would be for friends and family if the angelic trumpeter and head chorister had stuck to his heraldic beginnings and not become an electroacoustic composer working in the underground scene. Many parents make a huge investment of time and encouragement, but they shouldn't expect a soloist in return, rather a more complete person, enriched by the acquisition of a musical skill.

Of the 700 musicians who graduate from music college each year, only four per cent will find musical employment within the first three months. The handful who will make it as big-name soloists will probably have started on that route much earlier. The majority will never be able to make a full-time living from playing alone. However, although the profession is fiercely competitive – and standards have never been higher – musicianship is a skill that will travel. There are good orchestras across the country and throughout Europe. If you've really set your heart on playing in an orchestra or ensemble you'll probably succeed if you are prepared to travel.

But that is by no means the only option for graduates: everyone will at some time teach, and teaching can take many forms, from one-to-one lessons, to kindergarten groups, to class teaching, choir direction, adult education and community work. Teaching also feeds into regional music officer posts and inspectorates. You may be a pianist who chooses to accompany and ends up coaching singers, or a repetiteur helping in the opera studio. If you are a composer, teaching can reach new heights of creativity if you have the aptitude to be an animateur, leading group composing projects. Then there is music for special needs, music therapy and the multitude of therapies aimed at reducing musicians' stress: counselling, Alexander Technique, T'ai Chi.

For those who have already shown a bent for organisational skills at college, there is the realm of concert and artist management. Development or fund-raising posts are thick on the ground these days and are well suited to those who want to support music but have a head for business. Those going into arts management, or PR and marketing of music benefit hugely from a sound musical background and a real understanding of the demands of performance. Record production, broadcasting and sound engineering require acute listening skills, detailed repertoire knowledge and technical expertise.

Those who have studied music at university might consider writing: if you are passionate about your area and feel you have something to say, the world needs editors, researchers, broadcasters, programme-note and review writers. Music publishers need dedicated experts to work on composer's scores and on promoting their music. You may have language skills (always useful in music) and end up translating opera surtitles. This is not the place to detail how these professions operate, but to point out the enormous range of music-related careers.

We live in exciting times and the role of the musician is changing rapidly. Exponents of early music have begun to cross the boundaries between composer and performer once again, while schools are teaching improvisation. The musician is no longer a remote being, hiding behind the music stand or the works they create; the musicians of tomorrow are being equipped with the skills to communicate on every level to a multitude of different people. If you have travelled even a little way down the path into music you have done your part in ensuring its existence: for you will be the listener with open ears, and without such an audience music cannot live. *HW*

Useful Addresses

This listing relates to organisations and institutions which are mentioned in the book. General addresses/numbers are followed by:

- Choirs
- Choir schools
- Colleges/Universities
- Competitive festivals
- Composers
- Conservatoires
- County music services
- Examining boards
- GCSE/A-level boards
- Jazz/Rock
- Orchestras
- Pre-school music
- Scholarships
- School curriculum
- Specialist schools
- Summer courses
- Special needs
- Teaching organisations
- World music

- Further reading

Arts Council of England
14 Great St Peter St,
London SW1P 3NQ
Tel 0171 333 0100

Arts Council of Northern Ireland
185 Stranmillis Rd,
Belfast BT9 5DU
Tel 01232 381591

Arts Council of Wales
9 Museum Pl,
Cardiff CF1 3NX
Tel 01222 394711

Scottish Arts Council
12 Manor Pl,
Edinburgh EH3 7DD
Tel 0131 226 6051

Federation of Music Services
For information on local state music provision, from teachers to weekend music centres

and orchestras
Wheatley Hse,
12 Lucas Rd,
High Wycombe,
Bucks HP13 6QE
Tel 01494 439572

Incorporated Society of Musicians
Professional body for musicians including students. Has a list of teachers.
10 Stratford Pl,
London W1N 9AE
Tel 0171 629 4413

Musicians Union
60-62 Clapham Rd,
London SW9 0JJ
Tel 0171 582 5566

National Association for Gifted Children
Elder Hse,
Milton Keynes MK9 1LR
Tel 01908 673677

CHOIRS
British Choral Institute
Advisory, educational and promotional body
18 The Rotyngs,
Rottingdean,
Brighton BN2 7DX
Tel 01273 300894

British Federation of Young Choirs
37 Frederick St,
Loughborough,
Leics LE11 3BH
Tel 01509 211664

British Methodist Youth Choir
Age range 17-27
35 Westwood Rd,
Sutton Coldfield,
W Midlands B73 6UP
Tel 0121 353 5909

National Association of Choirs
21 Charmouth Rd,
Lower Weston,
Bath BA1 3LJ
Tel 01225 426713

National Youth Choir of Great Britain
Age range 16-21
PO Box 67,
Holmfirth,
Huddersfield
HD7 1GQ
Tel 01484 687023

National Youth Choir of Scotland and Chamber Choir
Age range 16-24
18 Polmont Pk,
Falkirk FK2 0XT
Tel 01324 711749

National Youth Choir of Wales
Age range 16-21
Welsh Amateur Music Federation,
9 Museum Pl,
Cardiff CF1 3NX
Tel 01222 394711

New London Children's Choir
Age range 8+
41 Aberdare Gdns,
London NW6 3AL
Tel 0171 625 4641

Royal School of Church Music
Cleveland Lodge,
Westhumble,
Dorking, Surrey
RH5 6BW
Tel 01306 877676

The Voices Foundation
Charity funding choir teacher training in primary schools
21 Earls Court Sq,
London SW5 9BY
Tel 0171 370 1944

CHOIR SCHOOLS
Choir Schools' Association
General information
The Minster School,
Deangate,
York YO1 2JA
Tel 01904 624900

COLLEGES/ UNIVERSITIES
Universities and Colleges Admissions Service
General enquiries
Fulton Hse,
Jessop Ave,
Cheltenham,
Glos GL50 3SH
Tel 01242 222444
See also Further reading

COMPETITIVE FESTIVALS (SELECTIVE LIST)
Aberdeen International Youth Festival
3 Nutborn Hse,
Clifton Rd,
London SW19 4QT
Tel 0181 946 2995

BBC Young Musicians
BBC Music & Arts,
EG30, Television Centre,
London W12 7RJ
Tel 0181 895 6143/4

British Federation of Festivals for Music, Dance and Speech
For information on competitive festivals in UK/Ireland
Festivals Hse,
198 Park La,
Macclesfield,
Cheshire SK11 6UD
Tel 01625 428297

Festival of British Youth Orchestras in Edinburgh and Glasgow
NAYO, Ainslie Hse,
11 St Colme St,
Edinburgh EH3 6AG
Tel 0131 539 1087

Harrogate International Youth Music Festival
Perform Europe (Incoming),
Deepdene Lodge,
Deepdene Ave,
Dorking,
Surrey RH5 4AZ
Tel 01306 744360

Music for Youth's National Festivals
102 Point Pleasant,
London SW18 1PP
Tel 0181 870 9624

West Sussex International Youth Music Festival
see Harrogate International Youth Music Festival)

Other competitions are listed in the British Music Yearbook

COMPOSERS
Society for the Promotion of New Music
Francis Hse,
Francis St,
London SW1P 1DE
Tel 0171 828 9696

Lloyds Bank Young Composers Workshop
BBC Young Musicians
BBC Music & Arts,
EG30, Television Centre,
London W12 7RJ
Tel 0181 895 6143/4

CONSERVATOIRES
Birmingham Conservatoire
University of Central England,
Paradise Pl,
Birmingham B3 3HG
Tel 0121 331 5901/2
junior department:
Tel 0121 331 5905

Guildhall School of Music and Drama
Silk St, Barbican,
London EC2Y 8DT
Tel 0171 628 2571
Junior department:
Tel 0171 382 7160

Leeds College of Music
Cookridge St,
Leeds LS2 8BH
Tel 0113 243 2491

London College of Music and Media,
Thames Valley University,
St Mary's Rd,
London W5 5RF

Tel 0181 231 2304
Junior department:
as above (also offers GCSE and A-level courses)

Royal Academy of Music
Marylebone Rd,
London NW1 5HT
Tel 0171 873 7373
Junior department:
Tel 0171 873 7380

Royal College of Music
Prince Consort Rd,
London SW7 2BS
Tel 0171 589 3643
Junior department:
Tel 0171 591 4334

Royal Northern College of Music
124 Oxford Rd,
Manchester M13 9RD
Tel 0161 273 6283
Junior department:
as above

Royal Scottish Academy of Music and Drama
100 Renfrew St,
Glasgow G2 3DB
Tel 0141 332 4101
Junior department:
as above

Trinity College of Music
11-13 Mandeville Pl,
London W1M 6AQ
Tel 0171 935 5773
Junior department:
as above

Welsh College of Music and Drama
Castle Grounds,
Cathays Pk,
Cardiff CF1 3ER
Tel 01222 342854
Junior department:
Tel 01222 394665

COUNTY MUSIC SERVICES
Federation of Music Services
For information on local state music provision, from teachers to weekend music centres and orchestras
Wheatley Hse,
12 Lucas Rd,

High Wycombe,
Bucks HP13 6QE
Tel 01494 439572

EXAMINING BOARDS
Associated Board of the Royal Schools of Music
14 Bedford Sq,
London WC1B 3JG
Tel 0171 636 5400

Birmingham Conservatoire
University of Central England,
Paradise Pl,
Birmingham B3 3HG
Tel 0121 331 5912

Guildhall School of Music and Drama
Examinations Service,
Dept of Initial Studies,
Silk St, Barbican,
London EC2Y 8DT
Tel 0171 382 7167

Independent Contemporary Music Awards
PO Box 134, Witney,
Oxon OX8 7FS
Tel 07000 780728

London College of Music Examinations
Thames Valley University,
St Mary's Rd,
London W5 5RF
Tel 0181 231 2364

National College of Brass
242 Grimsby Rd,
Cleethorpes,
Lincs DN35 7EY
Tel 01472 691623

National College of Music
4 Duffield Rd,
Chelmsford CM2 9RY
Tel 01245 354596

Royal College of Music
Prince Consort Rd,
London SW7 2BS
Tel 0171 589 3643

Royal College of Organists
7 St Andrew St,
London EC4A 3LQ
Tel 0171 936 3606

Trinity College of Music (Exams)
16 Park Crescent,
London W1N 4AP
Tel 0171 323 2328

GCSE/A-LEVEL
Assessment and Qualifications Alliance (AQA, incl. Northern Examinations Board)
Devas St,
Manchester M15 6EX
Tel 0161 953 1180

Edexcel Foundation London Exams
32 Russell Sq,
London WC1B 5DN
Tel 0171 393 4444
For publications:
Edexcel Publications,
Bellamy Rd,
Mansfield,
Notts NG18 4LN
Tel 01623 467467

Oxford and Cambridge Schools Examining Board (part of OCR)
Purbeck Hse,
Purbeck Rd,
Cambridge CB2 2PU
Tel 01223 411211

Scottish Qualifications Authority
Ironmills Rd, Dalkeith
Midlothian EH22 1LE
Tel 0131 663 6601

Southern Examining Group (SEG)
GCSE only
Central Administration
Office, Stag Hill Hse,
Guildford GU2 5XJ
Tel 01483 506506

Welsh Joint Education Committee
245 Western Ave,
Cardiff CF5 2YX
Tel 01222 265000

JAZZ AND ROCK
Academy of Contemporary Music
Haydon Pl,
Guildford GU1 4LR
Tel 01483 456788

Music Education Guide

Birmingham Institute of Guitar
Queen's Chambers,
Old Snow Hill,
Birmingham B4 6HX
Tel 0121 212 1989

Guildhall Summer School
Guildhall School of
Music and Drama,
Silk St, Barbican,
London EC2Y 8DT
Tel 01702 714733

Jazz Academy Vacation Courses
12 Castle St,
Berkhamsted,
Herts HP4 2BQ
Tel 01442 864989

Jazz Services
National database on
jazz in education
Rm 518, Africa Hse,
64 Kingsway,
London WC2B 6BD
Tel 0171 405 0737

Liverpool Institute for Performing Arts
Mount St,
Liverpool L1 9HF
Tel 0151 330 3002

National Youth Jazz Orchestra of Scotland
Age range 12-21
(see National Youth
Orchestra of Scotland)

National Youth Jazz Orchestra of Great Britain
Age range 11-25
11 Victor Rd,
Harrow HA2 6PT
Tel 0181 863 2717

Powerhouse Rock Schools
74 Stanley Gdns,
London W3 7SD
Guitar Institute &
Basstech:
Tel 0181 740 1031
Drumtech,
Keyboardtech
& Vocaltech:
Tel 0181 749 3131

Registry of Guitar Teachers
122 Endeavour Way,
Croydon CR0 4TR
Tel 0181 665 7666

Rock School/Trinity Graded Examinations for Guitar, Bass and Drums
Rock School Ltd,
Broomfield Rd,
Richmond,
Surrey TW9 3HS
Tel 0181 332 6303

ORCHESTRAS
Britten-Pears Orchestra and Baroque Orchestra
Age range 18+
Britten-Pears School for
Advanced Musical
Studies, High St,
Aldeburgh, Suffolk
IP15 5AX
Tel 01728 452935

ESO Youth Orchestra
Age range up to 21
Rockcliffe Hse,
40 Church St, Malvern,
Worcs WR14 2AZ
Tel 01684 560696

European Union Youth Orchestra
Age range 14-23
6a Pont St,
London SW1X 9EL
Tel 0171 235 7671

Jewish Youth Orchestra of Great Britain
Age range 13-18
5 Bradby Hse,
Carlton Hill,
London NW8 9XE
Tel 0171 624 1796

London Philharmonic Youth Orchestra
Age range 18-26
35 Doughty St,
London WC1N 2AA
Tel 0171 546 1600

London Schools Symphony Orchestra
Age range 14-18
Centre for Young
Musicians,
Morley College,
61 Westminster Bridge
Rd,
London SE1 7HT
Tel 0171 928 3844

National Association of Youth Orchestras
Ainslie Hse,
11 St Colme St,
Edinburgh EH3 6AG
Tel 0131 539 1087

National Children's Chamber Orchestra of Great Britain
Age range 10-16
The Bourne,
20 Salisbury Ave,
Harpenden,
Herts AL5 2QG
Tel 01582 760014

National Children's Orchestra
Age range 7-13
157 Craddocks Ave,
Ashstead,
Surrey KT21 1NU
Tel 01372 276857

National Children's Orchestra of Scotland
Age range 8-14
(see National Youth
Orchestra of Scotland)

National Youth Music Theatre Orchestra
Age range 11+
Fifth flr, Palace Theatre,
Shaftesbury Ave,
London W1V 8AY
Tel 0171 734 7478

National Youth Orchestra of Great Britain
Age range 10-19
Causeway Hse,
Lodge Causeway,
Bristol BS16 3HD
Tel 0117 965 0036

National Youth Orchestra of Scotland
Age range 12-21
13 Somerset Pl,
Glasgow G3 7JT
Tel 0141 332 8311

National Youth Orchestra of Wales
Age range up to 21
Welsh Joint Education
Committee,
245 Western Ave,
Cardiff CF5 2YX
Tel 01222 265247

Young Musicians' Symphony Orchestra
Age range 18-25
11 Gunnersbury Ave,
London W5 3NJ
Tel 0181 993 3135

PRE-SCHOOL MUSIC
British Kodály Academy
13 Midmoor Rd,
London SW19 4JD
Tel 0181 946 6528

British Suzuki Institute
39 High St,
Wheathampstead,
Herts AL4 8BB
Tel 01582 832424

Colourstrings/ Colourkeys
c/o The Szilvay
Foundation,
4 Ullswater Cl,
London SW15 3RF
Tel 0181 547 3073

Kodály Institute of Britain
133 Queen's Gate,
London SW7 5LE
Tel 0171 823 7371

Monkey Music Ltd
A music kindergarten
chain for children aged
six months to four years
8 Idmiston Rd,
London SE27 9HG
Tel 0181 761 7271

National Childbirth Trust
Information on local
music groups for
toddlers etc.
Alexandra Hse,
Oldham Tce,
London W3 6NH
Tel 0181 992 8637

SCHOLARSHIPS
Music Awards at Independent Senior Schools
See Further reading

SCHOOL CURRICULUM
School Curriculum and Assessment Authority
Reviews the national
curriculum, exams and
assessment for
maintained schools in
England and provides
information
Newcombe Hse,
45 Notting Hill Gate,
London W11 3JB
Tel 0171 229 1234

SPECIALIST SCHOOLS

Association of Music and Ballet Schools
Wells Cathedral School,
Wells, Somerset BA5 2ST
Tel 01749 672117

Chetham's School of Music
Long Millgate,
Manchester M3 1SB
Tel 0161 834 9644

City of Edinburgh Music School
Broughton High School,
Carrington Rd,
Edinburgh EH4 1EG
Tel 0131 332 7805

Music School of Douglas Academy
Mains Estate, Milngavie,
Glasgow G62 7HL
Tel 0141 956 2281

Pimlico School
Lupus St,
London SW1V 3AT
Tel 0171 828 0881

Purcell School
Aldenham Rd, Bushey,
Herts WD2 3TS
Tel 01923 331100

St Mary's Music School
Coates Hall,
25 Grosvenor Crescent,
Edinburgh EH12 5EL
Tel 0131 538 7766

Wells Cathedral School Music School
Wells, Somerset BA5 2ST
Tel 01749 672117

Yehudi Menuhin School
Cobham Rd, Stoke
d'Abernon, Cobham,
Surrey KT11 3QQ
Tel 01932 864739

SUMMER SCHOOLS AND COURSES

(selective list)

Andover Harp Course
Residents 14-25;
non-residents 12-14
44 Church Crescent,
London N3 1BJ
Tel 0181 349 4067

Beauchamp House Holiday Music Courses
Age range 8+
Churcham,
Gloucester GL2 8AA
Tel 01452 750382

Benslow Music Trust
Over 100 weekend and
residential courses
Little Benslow Hills,
off Benslow La, Hitchin,
Herts SG4 9RB
Tel 01462 459446

Canford Summer School of Music
5 Busby Cl,
Old Barn La, Kenley,
Surrey CR8 5AU
Tel 0181 660 4766

Dartington International Summer School
Dartington Hall,
Totnes,
Devon TQ9 6DE
Tel 01803 865988

Double Bass Summer School
Age range 8-25
7 St Clair Dv,
Worcester Park,
Surrey KT4 8UG
Tel 0181 330 3188

Gathering of the Clans
Age range 14+
The Villa, Tollerson,
York YO6 2EQ
Tel 01347 838273

HF Holidays Ltd
Children must have
a parent/guardian
Imperial Hse,
Edgware Rd,
London NW9 5AL
Tel 0181 905 9556

Llandaff Summer Music Course
Age range 10-17
50 Parc-y-Coed,
Creigiau,
Cardiff CF4 8LY
Tel 01222 892388

Marlborough College Summer School
Marlborough,
Wilts SN8 1PA
Tel 01672 892388

Musicale Holidays
The Bourne,
20 Salisbury Ave,
Harpenden,
Herts AL5 2QG
Tel 01582 460978

National Children's Music Camps
61 Crown Rd,
Sutton SM1 1RT
Tel 0181 715 4048

Pro Corda Trust
National School for
Young Chamber Music
Players
Leiston Abbey Hse,
Theberton Rd, Leiston,
Suffolk IP16 4TB
Tel 01728 831354

Oundle International Festival and Summer School for Young Organists
Age range 14-23
The Old Crown,
Glapthorn, Oundle,
Peterborough PE8 5BJ
Tel 01832 272026

Oxford Cello School
67 Oxford Rd,
Abingdon,
Oxon OX14 2AA
Tel 01235 530572

Scottish Amateur Music Association
18 Craigton Crescent,
Alva,
Clackmannanshire
FK12 5DS
Tel 01259 760249

Sing for Pleasure
(all ages)
25 Fryerning La,
Ingatestone,
Essex CM4 0DD
Tel 01277 353691

Other summer schools
and courses are listed in
the British Music
Yearbook

SPECIAL NEEDS

Arts for Health
Information and advice
for those seeking arts as
part of health care
Manchester
Metropolitan University,
All Saints,
Manchester M15 6BY
Tel 0161 236 8916

British Society for Music Therapy
25 Rosslyn Ave,
East Barnet,
Herts EN4 8DH
Tel 0181 368 8879

National Association for Special Education Needs
Promotes development
of children with special
needs
NASEN Hse,
4-5 Amber Business
Village, Amber Cl,
Amington, Tamworth,
W Midlands B77 4RP
Tel 01827 311500

Sound Sense
Information on music
and disability
Riverside Hse,
Rattlesden,
Bury St Edmunds,
Suffolk IP30 0SF.
Tel 01449 736287

TEACHER ASSOCIATIONS

Association of Woodwind Teachers
90 Becmead Ave,
Kenton,
Middx HA3 8HB
Tel 0181 907 8428

British Kodály Academy
13 Midmoor Rd,
London SW19 4JD
Tel 0181 946 6528

British Suzuki Institute
39 High St,
Wheathampstead,
Herts AL4 8BB
Tel 01582 832424

Colourstrings/ Colourkeys
c/o The Szilvay
Foundation,
4 Ullswater Cl,
London SW15 3RF
Tel 0181 547 3073

Dalcroze Society
Musical education
through movement
41a Woodmansterne
Rd, Coulsdon,
Surrey CR5 2DJ
Tel 0181 645 0714

European Piano Teachers' Association
1 Wildgoose Dv,
Horsham,
W Sussex RH12 1TU
Tel 01403 267761

European String Teachers Association
247 Hay Green La,
Bournville,
Birmingham B30 1SH
Tel 0121 475 3345

Kodály Institute of Britain
133 Queen's Gate,
London SW7 5LE
Tel 0171 823 7371

Incorporated Society of Musicians
Professional body for musicians including students; has a list of teachers
10 Stratford Pl,
London W1N 9AE
Tel 0171 629 4413

National Association of Percussion Teachers
138 Springbank Rd,
London SE13 6SU
Tel 0181 698 7885

Registry of Guitar Teachers
122 Endeavour Way,
Croydon CR0 4TR
Tel 0181 665 7666

UNIVERSITIES
See Colleges

WORLD MUSIC
Asian Music Circuit
Unit F, West Point,
33-34 Warple Way,
London W3 ORG
Tel 0181 742 9911

Badejo Arts
African music and dance; annual summer school
Harmood Community Centre, 1 Forge Pl,
Ferdinand St,
London NW1 8DQ
Tel 0171 482 4292

Bharatiya Vidya Bhavan
Centre for Indian culture
4a Castletown Rd,

London W14 9HQ
Tel 0171 381 3086

Drum Call
Promotes African drumming
84 Bank Side St,
Leeds LS8 5AD
Tel 0113 248 6746

Ray Man
Musical instrument shop/Chinese centre
29 Monmouth St,
London WC2H 9DD
Tel 0171 240 1776

Rotterdam Conservatorium
P. de Hoochweg 222,
3024 BJ Rotterdam,
Netherlands
Tel +31 10 476 73 99

School of Oriental and African Studies
Thornhaugh St,
Russell Sq,
London WC1H 0XG
Tel 0171 637 2388

South Bank Centre gamelan programme
Gamelan co-ordinator,
Royal Festival Hall,
London SE1 8XX
Tel 0171 921 0848

Steel Band Adviser
60 Greenford Gdns,
Greenford,
Middx UB6 9LZ
Tel 0181 578 6485

UK-Japan Music Society
27 Heron Cl,
Great Glen,
Leicester LE8 9DZ
Tel 0116 259 3891

FURTHER READING

A Basis for Music Education
by Keith Swanwick
Routledge (£12.99)

Boarding Schools and Colleges 1998
John Catt Educational,
tel 01728 663666
(£9.95)

British Music Yearbook
Rhinegold Publishing,
tel 0171 333 1721
(£23.95)

British Performing Arts Yearbook
Rhinegold Publishing,
tel 0171 333 1721
(£23.95)

Careers in Music
by John Westcombe
Heinemann (£10.50)

Choosing your Independent School
ISIS, tel 0171 630 8793
(£8.50)

CRAC Degree Course Guides (£4.99 each)
Directory of Further Education (£69.50)
Which Degree?
(£19.99 each; on CD-ROM)
Which University?
(£58)
Hobson's Publishing, tel 01223 354551

Getting into Music, Drama and Dance
Trotman & Co Ltd, distr.
Bailey, tel 01797 369961 (£7.99)

Good Schools Guide
Ebury Press, tel 0171 973 9690 (£10.99)

Handbook of Music Awards and Scholarships
Musicians Benevolent Fund, tel 0171 636 4481 (£3.50)

How to Choose your Degree Course
Trotman & Co Ltd, distr.
Bailey, tel 01797 369961 (£14.99)

It's Your Choice
A guide to choosing at 16+
DfEE, PO Box 6927
London E3 3NZ
Tel 0845 602 2260
(free)

Making Music with the Young Child with Special Needs
by Amanda Little
Jessica Kingsley
Publishers, tel 0171 833 2307 (£7.99)

Music, Mind and Education
by Keith Swanwick
Routledge (£11.99)

Music Awards at Independent Senior Schools
Music Masters' and Mistresses' Association,
tel 01892 890537
(£7.99)

Music Education Yearbook
Listings of all aspects of musical education
Rhinegold Publishing,
tel 0171 333 1721
(£16.50)

National Directory of Instrumental Teachers
Musicians Union, tel 0171 582 5566 (a free list of local teachers is available)

Parents' Guide to Higher Education
UCAS, tel 01242 222444 (free)

The Pocket Practice Book
by Diana Tickell
Pit Pat Publishing,
28 Patshull Rd,
London NW5 2JY

The Times Good University Guide
Times Books/
HarperCollins (£8.99)